THIS IS LIVING

THIS IS
LIVING

DAILY INSPIRATION
TO LIVE YOUR FAITH

RICK MCDANIEL

Fedd Books
P.O. Box 341973
Austin, TX 78734
www.thefeddagency.com

Published in association with The Fedd Agency, Inc., a literary agency.

ISBN: 978-1-949784-85-5
eISBN: 978-1-949784-83-1
Library of Congress Number: 2021918595

Cover Design: Deryn Pieterse
Cover Image: Steve Johnson

Printed in the United States of America

First Edition 22 23 24 25 / 9 8 7 6 5 4 3 2 1

TO MY DAD,
who has lived his faith with incredible
commitment for more than sixty years.

CONTENTS

INTRODUCTION

About seven years ago, Salem Communications approached me about writing a weekly devotional. My first response was to take a pass. I felt as if I didn't have time in my schedule to add another responsibility, especially something as time-consuming as writing.

But Salem's Dave Jackson is a persuasive fellow. He convinced me that I could use material from my years of preaching and writing. He told me it would be fairly easy and would not take too much time. So I began writing a weekly devotional that was sent out every Wednesday by Salem.

At first, I did just use previous material from my books. As time passed, though, I began to see new possibilities. I have traveled many places and have seen many amazing things during my life. I have been to all fifty states in America and more than thirty countries. Along the way, I have heard some great stories from tour guides, park rangers, ministry friends, and others.

I would hear or read a story, and my mind would begin to think about a spiritual truth. Years of studying and preaching the Bible meant I had knowledge and the ability to extract spiritual truths from fascinating stories. The more I trained myself to think this way, the more material I produced.

At the same time, I was having everyday experiences that revealed deeper spiritual truths. I would write about them, as well as about lesser-known passages of Scripture that had enlightening messages.

I knew this could lead to a devotional book over time. I began to catalog the best of these devotions, knowing that the time would come when I would have enough to share in a book.

Stories are the fabric of life; people love when stories are told in a compelling way. Great stories combined with biblical truths can powerfully minister to people.

The purpose of this devotional book is to share stories and truths that inspire people to more impactfully live out their Christian faith. Reading a devotion every day for one hundred days can help you put biblical principles into practice on a daily basis. Your spiritual life will be positively enriched, and I pray that this will encourage your personal spiritual growth.

Stories from nature, stories about famous places, and stories from everyday life are all included here. Journeys around America and around the world fill the pages. It is my hope and prayer that the words of inspiration and challenge will give you a daily biblical boost.

THIS IS **LIVING**

YOUR TIME WILL COME

Let us not become weary in doing good.
—**GALATIANS 6:9** (NIV)

Visiting the Louvre in Paris was almost overwhelming to me. The sheer size of the museum, as well as the vast number of famous artworks, is remarkable. However, only one piece of art had its own room. Only one painting had a long line of people waiting to view it: the *Mona Lisa*.

The *Mona Lisa* is a work of art that has captured the imagination of humanity for more than five hundred years. The mysterious smile, the penetrating eyes, and the overall air of mystique surrounding the *Mona Lisa* cannot easily be explained. It is more than just a supreme example of Renaissance art. It also encapsulates a unique spirit.

There is something about it that draws people in. The painting is a visual representation of the idea of happiness. It is a quintessential example of how art is not easily explained, and as the old-time preacher would say, "It is more felt than tell."

The *Mona Lisa* may now be the world's most famous work of art, but for most of its life it was relatively obscure. Painted by

Leonardo da Vinci in 1503, it was not recognized as a masterpiece until the beginning of the twentieth century. As late as the 1850s, Leonardo was believed to be far inferior to fellow Renaissance artists Titian and Raphael, whose paintings were worth far more money than the *Mona Lisa*.

It wasn't until it was stolen in the summer of 1911 that it would capture the attention of the general public. Newspapers spread the story of the crime worldwide. When the painting was finally returned to the Louvre two years later, its fame was worldwide. Could Leonardo da Vinci have predicted that it would take four centuries for his masterpiece to be appreciated?

What about you? Have you ever wondered why some things have not happened as you hoped? You have done what is right, but there are no results. You think that being faithful has simply not resulted in the blessings of God. Galatians 6:9 (NIV) tells us, *Let us not become weary in doing good, for at the proper time we will reap a harvest if we do not give up.*

Have you been serving others and helping those in need? Have you been doing as Jesus taught us by loving others more than yourself? Maybe there are desires in your heart—hopes that are not being realized. Perhaps you believe that no matter how hard you work, no one seems to notice.

Don't grow tired of doing good. Don't ever think that God isn't noticing your service. There will be a season when all your hard work will be recognized. God is making you into a masterpiece. Your time will come.

BE VIGILANT

Your enemy, the devil, is like a roaring lion, sneaking around
to find someone to attack.
—1 PETER 5:8

A few years ago, less than an hour after we landed in Milan,
Italy, my briefcase was stolen. I told my wife, Michelle, to
wait for a moment, and I walked up to a counter with our luggage
to purchase train tickets. I set my luggage and briefcase on the
ground.

When I was finished at the counter, I turned around and
saw that my briefcase was gone. The briefcase contained my new
laptop, my glasses, my sunglasses, a watch, my books, and all our
travel documents. In just a short period of time, in the first hour
of my vacation, I had been robbed.

I had never before been robbed in my entire life (well, besides
by various referees and officials during my sports career). I began
to think about how I had been warned over the years to look out
for gypsies who steal for a living in various European countries.

People are not supposed to steal; it is against the law to rob
someone. However, I had to bear some responsibility for what

had happened. I should never have turned my back and left my briefcase behind me where I could not see it. In fact, I should have brought it with me and left everything else with my wife.

As I sat on the train thinking about all of this, 1 Peter 5:8 came to mind: *Be on your guard and stay awake. Your enemy, the devil, is like a roaring lion, sneaking around to find someone to attack.*

We have an enemy who is after us. We must be vigilant. We must be on our guard. We must be aware of the enemy's devices. I should have been more vigilant. If I had been, my briefcase would not have been stolen.

No matter what the robber may have wanted to do, I could have thwarted it by being on my guard. I knew thieves were there, and I needed to be cognizant of it. To quote my army officer son whom we were there to visit, I needed "situational awareness." Thankfully, I was able to replace most of the key documents within a few days, but the robbery left its sting.

Even more seriously, our enemy, Satan, wants to rob us of the abundant life. He wants to kill your dreams and destroy God's plan for your life. You must be on guard. You need to be constantly aware of the enemy's schemes.

The enemy will attack at any time. He will try to tempt you, trick you, and have you believe lies instead of the truth. Be vigilant at all times. Never let your guard down.

EAGLE-EYE VISION

I run toward the goal, so that I can win the prize
of being called to heaven.
—**PHILIPPIANS 3:14**

I love eagles. I have a bronze eagle on my bookcase, a wooden eagle on my file cabinet, and I also have pictures of eagles. I'm not saying I picked my alma mater, Boston College, because they are the Eagles, but it may have helped me make my decision.

When my family and I visited Alaska, I learned even more about eagles. They are amazing birds. While in flight, they can spot a fish a mile away. Human beings have very good eyesight, but we could never see a fish in water like an eagle can. Their eyesight is eight times stronger than ours.

Just as impressive is what they do after they spot a fish. They can fly up to one hundred miles an hour to get their prey. Once they lock in, they are completely focused, and they act swiftly to capture their prey. When they lock their talons onto the fish, it is over. The eagle has won, and the fish is their food.

This is the reason we have the term "eagle-eye." An eagle has vision and focus, and we need that in our lives. Focus is powerful.

It is a mathematical reality. Wherever force is focused, its power increases. This is why a laser is such a potent tool. Whether used in the field of manufacturing or medicine, lasers make life better because of their precision and power.

Have eagle-eyed focus today. Paul said in Philippians 3:14, *I run toward the goal, so that I can win the prize of being called to heaven.* Don't allow distractions to keep you from what God has called you to do.

There are likely more distractions in our world than ever before. It is so easy to binge-watch hundreds of television programs or play hundreds of video games. We can spend countless hours on the Internet surfing an endless amount of content. There are very many other distractions as well.

However, it is focus that leads to impact. When we focus, we can accomplish so much more. We can actually see what others don't see—and when we see it, we must act. Like the eagle, we need to go after our goal with speed and determination.

We miss out on too much in life when we are not focused. When we are not looking, opportunities can pass us by. Whenever we are distracted, there is the potential of overlooking exactly what we have been working for and waiting to see!

Stay focused and keep watching—and when you see it, act.

GOD'S FIRE PLAN

I will refine them like silver and test them like gold.
—ZECHARIAH 13:9 (NIV)

I recently had an opportunity to visit the Mariposa Grove of Sequoia trees in California. The grove had been closed for three years while they did enhancements to protect the trees and improve the visitor experience. Being able to see the world's largest trees in person was simply amazing. Redwoods may be taller, but there is no larger tree than a Sequoia. A vehicle can easily be driven through the base of one of these trees.

The most unusual feature of the trees is the black burn marks on the base of them. Every tree has these marks, and for good reason. Fire is what helps the trees to grow. When fire burns the underbrush, the Sequoias grow. They actually thrive on the fire scars. The tree can live even if it is burned. The Sequoia can withstand fire because its bark is twenty-one inches thick. Only if the fire reaches the top of the tree will the tree die.

Even more remarkable is how new Sequoias are born. The only way there can be a new Sequoia is if a Sequoia tree's cone is opened and the seeds come out. There are up to 9,100 tiny seeds in just one cone, but the cone will only open with tremendous heat. It takes a fire to produce enough heat to cause the cone to open and the seeds to be released.

A Sequoia takes eight hundred years to reach full growth, and they live for up to two thousand years. Some of the trees I saw were around when Jesus walked the earth. However, they only grow and reach their full potential if there is fire. Most forests are destroyed by fire, but fire is what makes the Sequoias grow to be the biggest trees in the world.

Christ followers are like the Sequoia. We need fire to help us grow. Zechariah 13:9 (NIV) tells us, *This third I will put into the fire; I will refine them like silver and test them like gold.* Fire purifies whatever it touches. We need the fire of God to cleanse away anything in our lives that keeps us from being totally committed to Jesus. God's fire can burn away whatever is not pleasing to Him.

No one wants to be in the furnace, but the fire is needed for our growth. God wants us to grow to full maturity. He wants us to be huge spiritually. He wants us to have a long life of ministry for Him. Let the fire of God burn so hot that it makes you like gold— shining beautifully for God.

MIRACLE COUNTRY

In the towns where Jesus had worked most of his miracles, the
people refused to turn to God.

—MATTHEW 11:20

One of the most memorable experiences on my trip to the
Holy Land was sitting on the shore of the Sea of Galilee. We
had just toured Capernaum, where Jesus had based His ministry,
and then we went to the shoreline together.

We had a powerful time of praying for each other. I felt the
presence of God in a way I have rarely known. I was certain that
the significant need I was praying about would be answered by
God—even though it would take a miracle.

However, this was miracle country. At least thirty-three of Jesus'
miracles were performed in the region of Galilee. If there was ever a
place to believe God for a miracle, it would be where more miracles per
square mile had happened than any other place on Earth. I left there
feeling as if a burden had been lifted. I was thankful for partners in
prayer and full of faith in God's miracle-working power.

What is strange—even funny—about the Galilee is how it was
viewed in Jesus' time versus how I viewed it that day. Jesus was

from the lower Galilee, an area densely populated—partly because Herod the Great had resettled Jews from Judea there. Also, the region was prosperous with fertile lands, it was a crossroads of trade between Egypt and Damascus via the King's Highway, and it had a strong fishing industry.

Galilee was on the fringe of traditional Jewish life. It was a frontier between Hebraic and Greco-Roman worlds, and as a result, it was scorned by Judeans. They used the term "Galilean" as a synonym for fool, heathen, or sinner.

It was in Galilee that Jesus announced His ministry, recruited eleven of His disciples, and preached nineteen of His parables. The Galilee was the main area of Jesus' public ministry. He demonstrated that the gospel was for everyone, not just for the elite. Jesus chose to spend the bulk of His time in ministry with those living in the Galilee.

Unfortunately, there is little evidence that Jesus' message was established after He left. Matthew 11:20 tells us, *In the towns where Jesus had worked most of his miracles, the people refused to turn to God.* Chorazin, Bethsaida, and Capernaum were all in the Galilee, and Jesus judged them for not responding to His message, even after they had witnessed His miracles.

I have not yet witnessed my miracle, although I am confident I will. I believe in the message of Jesus; and now more than ever after having been to the Galilee myself, I am certain that He is the truth.

A COMPLETE TURNAROUND

They won't obey God, and they are too worthless to do
anything good.
—TITUS 1:16

One of the apostle Paul's most trusted associates was Titus.
He helped Paul in Corinth, and then he was sent to Crete to
bring order to the church there and establish leadership.

Crete is a large island in the Mediterranean Sea south of Greece.
It is probably the same place as ancient Caphtor, from where the
Philistines originated. It is famous for its civilization of Minoans,
who were the originators of Greek culture. It is also known for the
stories about King Minos and the Minotaur, the imaginary half-
bull, half-man monster.

The people of Crete were infamous for their sinful behavior.
They were notorious for their corruption and excess. Paul quoted
their own poet Epimenides, who had written hundreds of years
before: *The people of Crete always tell lies. They are greedy and lazy
like wild animals* (Titus 1:12).

Paul said about them in Titus 1:16, *They are disgusting. They
won't obey God, and they are too worthless to do anything good.*

In fact, the phrase "like a Cretan," describing someone whose behavior is bad, is a reference to these very people.

Titus certainly had his hands full in dealing with such a group of people, yet he did a great job in turning around a difficult situation. He fulfilled his gospel assignment well, for tradition holds that he was the first bishop of Crete. I was able to visit the lovely Church of Saint Titus in Heraklion, which is dedicated to his ministry.

Paul tells us in 2 Corinthians 8 that Titus was dependable and diligent. He dealt with tough situations on more than one occasion. He is a model for how to succeed under trying circumstances. When I went to Crete and the people found out I was a pastor, they told me that Crete is 99 percent Christian. What a turnaround! This place that was so immoral and godless is now almost entirely Christian.

Maybe you face a challenging situation and wonder if it is possible to turn it around. It can be hard to have hope when the circumstances are so intimidating—but look what happened to Titus in Crete. An entire country was changed and experienced an amazing turnaround.

God can help you just like He did with Titus. Be diligent and committed. Depend on God to do something that will bring about a complete turnaround for you. Years from now, you will look back and see how incredibly different your life is because you trusted God for your own turnaround.

THIS IS **LIVING**

A WORK IN PROGRESS

He who has begun a good work in you will complete it.
—PHILIPPIANS 1:6 (NKJV)

I had the opportunity to visit La Sagrada Familia (Holy Family Church) in Barcelona, Spain. It is an amazing sight to see. It is a church that really looks like no other in the world. This church is unique for its architecture but also for something else—it is not finished. Construction of the church has lasted for 141 years so far! Antoni Gaudí designed the church and worked on it for forty-six years. Shortly before his death in 1926, the first tower was completed. Seven more towers are now done, and another ten are in construction.

Gaudí's vision for the church was to inspire feelings of elevation that would invite people to worship God. He was a deeply devoted Christian who practiced his faith and incorporated it into everything about the building. He thought of himself as "God's architect."

He knew that his vision was huge and that the church would take time to build. The engineering design is substantial—with an unprecedented eighteen towers. Then there are the intricate façades filled with sculptures that tell the story of Jesus' life.

Construction stopped for twenty years during the Spanish Civil War, and then repairs had to be made due to damage to the inside of the church. Work resumed slowly as donations came in to continue building.

The inside of the church was finally finished in 2010, but the outside of the church is still not complete. The goal for completion is 2026—one hundred years after Gaudí's death.

Being under construction is a good way to understand our lives. We are all works in progress. Philippians 1:6 (NKJV) tells us, *He who has begun a good work in you will complete it.*

Sometimes we get frustrated with the pace of our progress or the rate of our accomplishments. We may wish we were further along than we are. It takes time for the work to be done in our lives. It often takes longer than we think it should. We can get frustrated at the slow pace of growth and wish for more.

There are times when we have setbacks. Illness strikes, loss hits us, and relationships end. We have to regroup and continue on the journey. Despite the failures, we must choose to persevere past the disappointments and through the pain.

It won't take you 141 years to come to completion, but for however long your life is, you will be under construction. You are becoming who God created you to be. Remain open to opportunities, keep persisting through problems, and stay committed to finishing your life well.

BE THE BEST YOU CAN BE

The last will be first, and the first will be last.
—MATTHEW 20:16

Getting up at 4:00 a.m. on a vacation is not normal. If you asked my wife, she might say something even less charitable. But we rose early that day for a special reason: we wanted to be the first people in America to see the sunrise that day.

At 1,530 feet, Cadillac Mountain in Maine's Acadia National Park is the highest point on the Atlantic Seaboard. Combined with being one of the easternmost points in America, it is the first place to see the sunrise in this country. We drove up early that morning to be the first people in the country to see the sunrise.

However, when we arrived at the top of the mountain, we could barely find a parking spot. During the next forty-five minutes, we would watch hundreds more people pour onto the granite summit. I was not going to be first, but I would be one of hundreds that day who would see the sunrise in America before most others. It put me in some pretty rare company, but it wasn't *first*.

There is nothing wrong with wanting to be first; someone has to be. Greatness is a worthy goal to pursue. When Jesus said in Matthew 20:16 (NIV), *The last will be first, and the first will be last*, He wasn't criticizing the desire to be first. He was teaching us about having a servanthood attitude. Jesus doesn't want us to act superior to others; He wants us to serve others. You can be the best and still not act like you're better than everyone else.

The reality is that we cannot all be first. Only one person can be first. We can't all be the best; otherwise "best" doesn't mean anything. What each of us *can* pursue is to be the best we can be. We can take the talents, gifts, and opportunities God places in our lives and do all we can to be our best.

The key is to pursue impact over outcome—because you can control impact, but you cannot control results. You can control impact because it is about doing the best you can with your resources. Outcomes are different because there are so many things beyond our control. We can do everything right, but others can mess it up; that is the unpredictability of outcome.

Sometimes the results just don't show the whole story. However, the impact will. You may not be acknowledged as the best or receive the first-place prize, but as long as you keep trying to be the best you can be, you will be first in what matters most.

FORWARD FOCUS

No one who puts a hand to the plow and looks back is fit for service in the kingdom of God.
—**LUKE 9:62** (NIV)

Years ago I visited Sydney, Australia, and took a tour to see that city's many beautiful sights. We then went up to a bluff and looked out at the Sydney Harbor Bridge and the famous Opera House.

I learned a lot about this fascinating country that is also a continent. As you may know, Australia was first settled as a penal colony. It was where England used to send its prisoners. That is not an auspicious beginning for a new country.

I also learned about their crest. The Commonwealth Coat of Arms is the formal symbol of Australia. It pictures two animals: the emu (a flightless bird) and the kangaroo. These animals were chosen because they share a characteristic that appealed to the Australian people.

Both the emu and the kangaroo can only move forward, not backward. The emu's three-toed foot causes it to fall if it tries to go backward, and the kangaroo is prevented from moving backward because of its large tail.

I thought of the words of Jesus in Luke 9:62 (NIV): *No one who puts a hand to the plow and looks back is fit for service in the kingdom of God.* When we choose to follow Jesus, we only move forward; we never go back. The past can never be changed. Holding on to guilt and regret accomplishes nothing positive. The Australian citizens intuitively knew this when they chose for the symbol of their country native animals that could never go backward but could only move forward.

Our focus should be on forward motion. Try balancing a bike by sitting on it; you cannot do it. However, if you start moving forward, you can balance it perfectly. Forward momentum is what God wants for us, and this is how we live in God's kingdom.

You don't look back; you only look ahead. You can't succeed if you don't try. You are guaranteed not to make any shot that you do not take. You will never see results unless you make an attempt.

Everyone fails and makes mistakes. Welcome to the human race. If we focus on our past, we cannot move forward. No one wants to stay in a situation of setback, but many people do. They drag around the past and fill themselves with guilt and shame.

Think of yourself as an emu or kangaroo—incapable of moving backward. You can only move forward into the bright, marvelous future God has planned for you.

THE TRUE OLD FAITHFUL

If we are not faithful, he will still be faithful. Christ cannot deny
who he is.
—2 TIMOTHY 2:13

I visited Yellowstone National Park during the COVID-19
pandemic. The park was open, and although services were
somewhat limited, there was still much to explore. There are
many incredible sites to see, such as the Grand Prismatic Spring,
Yellowstone Falls, and the Grand Canyon of Yellowstone.

But the granddaddy of them all is Old Faithful. It is the
signature feature of the park, the picture on their brochure, and the
most recognizable of all the many sites. If you don't see anything
else in Yellowstone, you have to watch Old Faithful erupt.

I was able to watch it erupt five different times. We had a room
in the one wing of Old Faithful Inn that was still open. Our window
looked right out at the geyser. I saw it in the morning and at night.
I saw it erupt in different ways. But the one thing Old Faithful did
like clockwork was erupt. You could count on it going off about
every ninety minutes.

An Old Faithful eruption lasts from one and a half to five minutes and expels between 3,700 and 8,400 gallons of boiling water each time. Members of the Washburn Expedition of 1870 named the geyser for its consistent performance. Old Faithful is as spectacular and faithful today as it was 150 years ago.

Old Faithful faithfully erupts about every ninety minutes, but God is faithful every minute of every day. In fact, 2 Timothy 2:13 tells us, *If we are not faithful, he will still be faithful. Christ cannot deny who he is.* The very nature of God is faithfulness. The very character of Jesus is to always be faithful to us. Even when we are not faithful, He remains faithful. He is the true Old Faithful.

Where do we turn for help? Who can give us the strength we desperately need when life is so tough? Who can provide the hope that things will improve when there is no assurance of a better tomorrow? The answer is "Our faithful God."

We can count on Him when we see nothing but fear, chaos, and insecurity. When life is at its worst, He will take care of us. He always has and He always will. He will keep His promises. His faithfulness means that He will fulfill all His promises, and there are more than seven thousand of them in the Bible!

As I write, the world is still gripped in the throes of the COVID-19 pandemic. Indeed, these are trying times. But even in "normal" times, life is hard. Here is what I know for certain: when our stressful seasons are over, we can look back and reflect—and we will discover that God was faithful.

THIS IS **LIVING**

SEVEN SECONDS COULD DESTROY YOUR LIFE

Do not give the devil a foothold.
—**EPHESIANS 4:27** (NIV)

It took only seven seconds. University Hall in Charlottesville, Virginia, had stood for more than fifty years, but it was gone in seven seconds. U-Hall, as it was known, was the home of the University of Virginia basketball teams, and it housed offices and locker rooms for most of the school's other sports.

The clamshell dome roof and everything in the building were demolished in just a few seconds. There were 549 pounds of explosives and more than 3,200 lineal feet of detonating cord. Charges were set up in 468 locations around the columns and ring beam that held up the dome.

Once detonated, more than a dozen explosions could be heard, followed by a pause and then another loud set of blasts. The east side of the dome collapsed first. A second or two later, the west side came down. The entire demolition lasted seven seconds.

The arena where Ralph Sampson (the only three-time college basketball national player of the year) had played his career was destroyed. Many great games had been played, many great moments had occurred, and many great memories had taken place at U-Hall—but now the arena was gone.

The demolition was actually an implosion; the building collapsed from within. The reality is that the same thing can happen to us in the life we have built. It can be destroyed in just a moment. We can literally implode from within by bad choices or actions.

Ephesians 4:27 (NIV) says, *Do not give the devil a foothold.* An example of a foothold is when a person sticks his foot against the bottom of a door so the door cannot be closed. In using his foot to prevent you from closing the door, he has gained a "foothold."

One stupid action or one foolish decision can give the enemy a foothold in your life. If the enemy can get a foothold in your life, it won't be good for you. It gives the enemy the opportunity to eventually break into your life. Once he does, the result is destruction—and it can happen in seconds.

All the good you have done, all the ways you have helped others, and all your godly actions can be eviscerated by seven seconds of sinfulness. It may be hard to hear, but it is true.

Guard your heart from wrong emotions, make honesty your policy, and flee from sexual temptation. Resist pride, fight greed, and welcome servanthood. Stay close to Jesus and be led by the Holy Spirit.

Do not allow the enemy to destroy your life.

THIS IS LIVING

FOUR HUNDRED YEARS OF FAITHFULNESS

Now it is required that those who have been given a trust must prove faithful.

—1 CORINTHIANS 4:2 (NIV)

I recently visited Oberammergau, Germany, where the Passion Play is held every ten years. The story of the Passion Play is incredible, and it should be known by everyone.

In 1633 the bubonic plague was spreading throughout Europe. One in three Europeans died during the "Black Death" from the plague. When the plague hit the small Bavarian village of Oberammergau, eighty people died. The villagers got together and prayed, asking God to spare their village. They committed to sharing the story of Jesus' passion every ten years if God answered their prayer. Not one more villager died from the plague!

So the next year, 1634, they held their first Passion Play at the cemetery where the victims had been buried. The play tells the story of the last days of Jesus' life, from His entrance into Jerusalem to His resurrection. The people of Oberammergau have held the play every ten years ever since. For nearly four hundred years, these people have stayed faithful to their commitment.

The miracle God did was amazing, and so has been the faithfulness of these villagers. Only twice has the play not been held. The government banned it once, and it was also not held during World War II. Both were circumstances out of the villagers' control. Even more amazing is that everyone who is in the play must be from Oberammergau—and there are two thousand actors!

The play is held at the beginning of every decade. There are five performances each week for five months from May to October. The play lasts for eight hours, and it includes a dinner break.

The village is small and the roads are narrow. It is an out-of-the-way place in the middle of Bavaria, yet the tickets go on sale two years in advance, and they expect to sell out. More than half a million people will see the play, and all because a commitment was made to God in prayer that has been honored for nearly four hundred years.

First Corinthians 4:2 (NIV) says, *Now it is required that those who have been given a trust must prove faithful.* Have you made a commitment to God? Did you do it in prayer like the villagers, and did God come through for you too?

Maybe you made another kind of commitment to Jesus. Have you been faithful to it? Let the people of Oberammergau be your inspiration. If they can remain faithful for nearly four centuries, you can certainly be faithful to your commitments.

A BEAUTIFUL FAITH

He has made everything beautiful in its time. He has also set eternity in the human heart.
—ECCLESIASTES 3:11 (NIV)

I enjoy visiting art museums. Art inspires me. It lifts me and shows me what is possible. I have visited some of the greatest art museums in the world. I have been to the Hermitage in St. Petersburg, Russia, the Metropolitan in New York City, the Rijksmuseum in Amsterdam, the Vatican museum in Rome, and the Louvre in Paris.

One of the constants in all art—except contemporary art—is the religious theme. Michelangelo, da Vinci, Rembrandt, and many others focused their work on biblical stories or themes. Michelangelo's *The Creation of Adam*, da Vinci's *The Last Supper*, and Rembrandt's *Descent from the Cross* are all incredibly famous—and they are artistic representations of biblical truth.

The Vatican is especially filled with Christian art. The paintings, sculptures, and tapestries communicate biblical themes with phenomenal beauty.

To truly view these classic works as the artists intended, they must not be seen as simply paintings or sculptures, nor should they be viewed as mere relics of religious history. Rather, they are intended to reflect a living, timeless faith.

When I was in the Sistine Chapel, it was packed with people in the middle of the day during the middle of the week. The paintings are breathtaking, but the truth they present is even more so. The scene of hell is one that should make any person shudder.

Michelangelo's *Pieta* in St. Peter's Basilica is heartbreaking. The pain of Mary as she holds her dead son, Jesus, is impossible to miss. This is art at its very best. It moves us to consider transcendent truth, and there is no greater truth than the biblical message.

Most Christian visual art today is created for media (cable, streaming apps, etc.) and movies. These distribution channels have become the predominant medium for Christian artists. It is certainly more accessible than other forms of art. However, if the great artists no longer create religious art, then these museums become even more significant. They hold a treasure that Christ followers need to pursue.

Ecclesiastes 3:11 (NIV) tells us, *He has made everything beautiful in its time. He has also set eternity in the human heart.* My hope is that the thousands who see this art in museums all over the world every single day are being impacted by it.

I pray that the truth displayed will touch their hearts and open them up to the transforming power of the gospel, that we all would come to a personal, living faith through our exposure to such powerful expressions of Christ's love—and not just gain mere historical knowledge.

ARE YOU A DECOY?

Even though they will make a show of being religious,
their religion won't be real.
—2 TIMOTHY 3:5

My father loves to hunt. All throughout my growing-up years, he was either talking about hunting, planning a hunting trip, or actually hunting. He loved all kinds of hunting, especially fowl. He loved hunting grouse, pheasant, and duck. He even had a hunting dog.

Teddy was a Chesapeake Bay Retriever. My dad grew up on the eastern shore of Maryland near the Chesapeake Bay, so he loved that dog. Teddy would retrieve what Dad shot down. He was a great swimmer, had a coat made to repel water, and had a mouth that had a large space between teeth where he could hold a duck.

In our home, my dad kept all his hunting gear in the basement. He had a gun safe, a bench where he made his own ammunition, and a closet with all his hunting clothes. He also had his duck decoys. Those decoys were remarkably lifelike. If you didn't know you were in a basement, you might think those ducks were real.

When Dad went hunting, he put the decoys out in the water. Sure enough, the ducks would come around. Dad never wanted to shoot a duck in the water. He waited until they flew away, and then he shot them down—or at least tried to. He thought the fun was in trying to hit a moving target. When he was successful, the duck would fall out of the sky into the lake. Teddy would then swim out, pick up the duck, and bring it back to Dad.

I have interacted with all kinds of people through the years, and I often think about those decoys. They looked just like ducks. They were the right size, they had the proper coloring, and they floated on the water—but they were not real ducks.

Some people I have met and known looked like real Christ followers, but they were just decoys. Acting religious does not equate to knowing and following Jesus.

Second Timothy 3:5 says, *Even though they will make a show of being religious, their religion won't be real.* It is a hard reality to face. Some people say they want to follow Jesus but then refuse to commit to Him. They are decoys.

This is not easy to digest, and it is hard to hear. It will give you a headache and heartache, but it is true.

Decoys are not alive. They look alive, and they float on the water just like the real thing, but they are not real. The question is this: Are you a decoy? Are you a fully devoted follower of Jesus Christ—or do you just look like one?

GOD PLEASER OR PEOPLE PLEASER

I am not trying to please people. I want to please God.
—GALATIANS 1:10

Healthy relationships require you to be a God pleaser more than a people pleaser. It may sound counterintuitive, but it is true. If you seek to please people more than God, you actually end up with unhealthy relationships. Galatians 1:10 tells us, *I am not trying to please people. I want to please God. Do you think I am trying to please people? If I were doing that, I would not be a servant of Christ.*

You can never please everyone. Accepting that you cannot make everyone happy helps your relationships; it doesn't harm them. Some people are driven to be liked, to want everyone to be happy, to have everyone get along. It may be great in theory, but in reality, everyone cannot always get along. People are never going to always agree. Two people can be in the same situation and see it in two completely different ways.

People pleasing ultimately leads to unhappiness. When your life is about pleasing other people who will never be fully satisfied, you will just be frustrated and unhappy. When you want to please people, you begin to conform your lifestyle to that of others because you fear rejection.

I recently had an interesting experience at the golf course. I decided at the last minute to play, and I really hadn't planned to play golf that week. I showed up as what they call a single—I didn't have a partner or group to play with. They put me in a group with three young guys.

They were talking in ways different from how people usually talk around me (as a pastor). They were talking about subjects I usually don't talk about, and they were consuming a fair amount of beer in the process. One of them actually hit me with a golf ball! The more I listened to these guys talk, the more I felt the pressure to conform.

That experience reminded me just how strong the pressure is to please people—to do what they are doing, to talk like they are talking, and to be like them. I wanted so much to tell them who I was, but I kept it a secret the whole time because it was a lot more fun.

If you are a people pleaser, you are going to conform your lifestyle to what pleases people—and you are not going to please God. If you are going to follow Christ, if you are going to be His servant, then you need to conform your lifestyle to the example and teachings of Jesus—not to the world.

BELIEVE GOD FOR THE IMPOSSIBLE

Nothing is impossible for God!
—LUKE 1:37

In Luke 1:34–38, the angel told Mary that she would have a son. Her response was, *How can this happen? I am not even married!* The angel's response was, *Nothing is impossible for God!* Mary simply replied, *Let it happen as you have said.*

Mary chose to believe that nothing was impossible with God. Her belief was rewarded when she conceived and Jesus was born. The most incredible miracle had occurred: God became man.

What seems impossible can become possible. What is it in your life that seems impossible at the moment? You must choose to believe. When you believe, the impossible becomes possible. For some people, miracles are hard to believe in. When we choose to believe, we open up the door to the miraculous. We position ourselves to see God make the impossible possible.

A New Yorker named Kevin Coughlin had been blind for twenty years. In August 2013, the thick white fog over his eyes began to lift, and he became able to see. Coughlin had a hereditary condition called Leber hereditary optic neuropathy that impairs and destroys optic nerve cells. Dr. Susan Fromer of Lenox Hill Hospital said, "I'm not aware of another case like this in medical history actually—a true optic neuropathy that resolved itself after twenty years."

"Resolved itself" is how doctors describe a miracle. They also use phrases like "spontaneous remission" when the impossible becomes possible. Coughlin simply said, "Now, I'm totally different. I'm a person who meditates daily. I pray."

Miracles happen in all kinds of ways and in all kinds of situations. In December 2016, there was a huge ten-alarm fire in Cambridge, Massachusetts, just outside of Boston. The fire destroyed fifteen structures, displacing almost eighty people—but no one was killed or even seriously injured. It was nothing short of a miracle.

Miracles come in all shapes and sizes. Sometimes we miss the miracle because we are looking for the ordinary rather than the extraordinary. Sometimes we miss it because we are not looking at all. Sometimes we refuse to acknowledge that what has happened is unexplainable except as miraculous.

This does not mean that your belief will immediately lead to a miracle. There may be problems or challenges that develop along the way. There will also likely be a waiting period that teaches you to trust. But the miracle will come.

So what do you need to believe for? Is it a health challenge, a financial issue, a marital problem, or something else? You can be like Mary and believe God for the impossible. The miracle of Jesus means that anything is possible.

BETTER THAN YOU ARE

For those God foreknew he also predestined to be conformed
to the image of his Son.
—ROMANS 8:29 (NIV)

James Michener became famous for his historical novels, like
Chesapeake, Hawaii, Centennial, and *Space.* He wrote forty
books that sold more than seventy-five million copies. His first
book was adapted as the popular musical *South Pacific* by Rodgers
and Hammerstein.

His novel *Hawaii* was published just as Hawaii became the
fiftieth state, garnering great interest. *Centennial* was about the
American West and was made into a twelve-part miniseries that
was shown on NBC. His books were based on extensive historical
and cultural research. Michener's style was characterized by people
fleshed out with deep genealogical and cultural roots.

Ironically, he was a man without a birth certificate. He did not
know when or where he was born. He never knew his biological
parents. Abandoned as an infant, he was raised as a foster son by a
widow, Mabel Michener.

For some unknown reason, Michener's accomplishments raised the ire of one of his adoptive family members. As Michener gained notoriety and fame, he began to receive hate-filled notes from this anonymous relative. The relative charged James with besmirching the Michener name, which he said he had no right to use. This continued even after Michener won the Pulitzer Prize for Fiction.

The words this hateful relative used that wounded Michener the most were, "Who . . . do you think you are, trying to be better than you are?" Michener wrote that those words were burned into his soul. He turned those negative words into a positive challenge. He even admitted to missing the nasty letters when his mysterious relative died. Michener said that he spent his entire life trying to be better than he was and that he was a brother to all who shared the same aspiration.

Are you trying to be better than you are? All followers of Christ should aspire to be the people God has called them to be. Romans 8:29 (NIV) tells us, *For those God foreknew he also predestined to be conformed to the image of his Son.* It is our destiny to be formed and shaped like Jesus.

To be better than you are means doing things you would not naturally do. It means not doing things you would naturally like to do. When we allow God's Spirit to work in us, we can become much better than we ever dreamed.

Of course, we will struggle and stumble as we try to be like Jesus, but in the process, we become better than we are.

THIS IS **LIVING**

BREAKING FREE

And immediately all the doors were opened
and everyone's chains were loosed.
—ACTS 16:26 (NKJV)

I had the privilege of visiting the ancient city of Philippi in Greece. This is the place where the apostle Paul founded the first Christian church in Europe. It is also here that the first person came to be a follower of Christ in Europe. Her name was Lydia, and she was saved and then baptized. I was actually able to visit the place where she was baptized in the Gangitis River.

Paul visited Philippi at least two other times. From Rome, he wrote the book of Philippians to this church. This book contains some of the most famous passages in the Bible (e.g., 1:6; 2:5–11; 3:12–14; 4:13). Paul's joy for the Philippian church is evident in his letter in which he encourages the Philippian Christians to live victorious Christian lives.

It was also in Philippi that Paul and Silas were beaten and arrested. I saw the jail where they were imprisoned. Paul cast a spirit of divination out of a woman, but when her masters realized they could no longer use her to make money, they dragged the two men before the rulers and accused them of being troublemakers.

Acts 16:25–26 (NKJV) tells us, *But at midnight Paul and Silas were praying and singing hymns to God. Suddenly there was a great earthquake, so that the foundations of the prison were shaken; and immediately all the doors were opened and everyone's chains were loosed.* A small earthquake happened at just that exact place and time. The power of God set them free from jail!

When this happened, the jailer drew his sword to kill himself since he assumed the prisoners had escaped. But Paul stopped him, and the jailer asked Paul, *What must I do to be saved?* Paul responded, *Believe on the Lord Jesus Christ, and you will be saved* (Acts 16:30–31 NKJV).

The same power of God is available today to anyone who needs it. People in prison are still being saved. In fact, there is a great movement of men and women who are being trained for ministry while in prison.

God still sets people free from every kind of bondage. Many people today have various addictions that keep them bound, such as alcohol, drugs, pornography, or overspending.

Let me assure you that if you are struggling with addiction or a life-controlling habit, God can set you free. The power of God is real, and it is available to everyone. Even if you have spent years bound in chains, God can set you free. What God did for Paul and Silas, He will do for you.

WE CAN'T BE IGNORED

By this everyone will know that you are my disciples, if you love
one another.
—JOHN 13:35 (NIV)

In AD 362, Roman emperor Julian recognized the amazing
benevolence of the Galileans toward strangers. The emperor,
who was known as "Julian the Apostate" because of his rejection
of Christianity, referred to Christians as "Galileans" since Galilee
was where Jesus was from and was where He conducted much of
His ministry.

Before Christianity, there was very little charity in the world,
but Christians followed Jesus' teaching to love their neighbors and
to help widows, orphans, the sick, and the disabled. As Jesus said
in John 13:35 (NIV), *By this everyone will know that you are my
disciples, if you love one another.*

Emperor Julian was struck by how Christians cared for the
poor and needy, but he was bothered by the fact that so many
people were converting to Christianity because of the loving
actions of Christians. Therefore, he decided to launch a campaign
to create pagan charities to match what the Christians were doing.

His campaign failed miserably. What would motivate people to sacrifice for others? Why would they spend their time helping others instead of focusing on themselves? They had no reason to do so, so they didn't. Only Christians cared for those in need.

What an amazing testimony to the impact of faithful Christ followers! The pagan emperor of the most powerful civilization in the world was so impressed that he wanted to replicate the charity of the Christians—but he couldn't do it.

All these years later, we find ourselves in a similar cultural moment. The challenge before us is to show God's love rather than just talk about it. I believe in the power of words, but the words must be backed up with action.

We live in an era when people are increasingly questioning the Christian faith. They are confused by educators who challenge faith and question biblical truth. They are disappointed by leaders who fail to live up to what they teach. They see hypocrisy, and they question whether what is being proclaimed is true.

What cannot be challenged, though, are loving acts of compassion. What cannot be denied is faithful commitment to those in need. Not only is God honored when Christians do good works, but it gets the attention of people.

The gospel must be preached. People need to know that they need a Savior. To get a hearing, though, we must show them before we can tell them. When we show God's love and compassion in practical ways, we earn the right to share about our faith.

THIS IS LIVING

ONE DAY AT A TIME

Do not conform to the pattern of this world,
but be transformed by the renewing of your mind.
—**ROMANS 12:2** (NIV)

I once heard John Maxwell say, "You will never change your life until you change something you do daily. The secret of your success is found in your daily routine." I believe this is absolutely true. I have seen in my own life the amazing accomplishments that result from a daily routine.

I have often joked publicly that I would be a very easy person to assassinate. I have such a consistent daily routine that it would not take long to figure out where I am each day and what I am doing. However, such a routine is the key to achieving my goals and seeing my dreams come true.

Would you like to change your life for the better? Can you imagine what it would be like if this year you experienced success like never before? I know it is possible—but where to begin?

How about reading the Bible daily for a year? Of the many changes you could make to your daily routine, there is nothing that can have more impact on you than this. Just one chapter each day will change your life.

It will change you because the Bible renews your mind. Romans 12:2 (NIV) says, *Do not conform to the pattern of this world, but be transformed by the renewing of your mind. Then you will be able to test and approve what God's will is—his good, pleasing and perfect will.*

When you read the Bible, you begin to think differently. Then you start acting differently. You live in a way in which doing God's will becomes natural to you. Over time, this literally transforms your life. You do not just change a little, but you become a new person.

As you read a chapter each day, you gain more wisdom. You simply become a wiser person. There is nothing more valuable than having wisdom for the many decisions you have to make. More important than just intellect or education, wisdom can bless your life in a myriad of ways.

You may think it is too time-consuming or difficult to read the Bible every day, but reading one chapter won't take very long. There are daily Bible-reading guides that include 365 chapters for the year, highlighting the overall message of God's Word. All you have to do is read a small portion each day.

Start reading today, even just one chapter. A few minutes a day will transform your life.

COMPLAINTS OR THANKS

Do all things without complaining.
—**PHILIPPIANS 2:14** (NKJV)

A man joined a monastery where the monks could only speak two words every seven years. After the first seven years passed, the novitiate met with the abbot, who asked him for his two words. "Food's bad," the man replied.

He then went back to spend another seven years before once again meeting with his ecclesiastical superior. "What are your two words now?" asked the priest. "Bed's hard," the man responded.

Seven years later, the man met with the abbot for the third time. "And what are your two words this time?" he was asked. "I quit" was the reply.

"I'm not surprised," answered the cleric. "All you've done since you got here is complain."

It is likely that we complain a bit more than once every seven years. In fact, complaining happens a lot—probably much more than we even realize.

Complaining is easy to do, but it is not good for us. Doctors have found that people who complain about their health diminish their role in recovery from illness, and they can actually worsen the symptoms of their disease.

Complaining hurts our relationships. People who complain frequently are labeled as whiners and can risk being excluded from social groups. They can end up losing friends because of their complaints.

Complaining is contagious. It drags conversations in a negative direction. Complaining begets complaining. It feeds on itself. This creates a loop where people feed off each other's negativity, draining them emotionally.

Not everything we talk negatively about is a complaint. If your computer is not working right and you call tech support to report the problem, that is not a complaint; but if you walk around the office telling everyone what a piece of junk your computer is, then you are complaining.

If complaining is so destructive, why do we complain? Many people complain to get attention. They use complaining as a means to draw attention to themselves.

Sometimes we complain as a way of connecting with others. It is a way of starting a conversation. We say, "It's only November. It shouldn't be this cold," but there are better ways to communicate. "What's good in your life today?" always works.

Philippians 2:14 (NKJV) tells us, *Do all things without complaining.* Accept the challenge to not complain and to improve your attitude, your outlook, and your life. When we stop complaining about what is missing in our lives and start being thankful for all we have, life changes for the better.

CONFORMING TO CULTURE

People who want to be rich fall into all sorts of
temptations and traps.
—1 TIMOTHY 6:9

Have you ever wanted to be on the top of the world? At 16,700 feet, La Rinconada, Peru, is the highest inhabited town on Earth. It is perched atop Mount Ananea in the Peruvian Andes, lying in the shadow of Bella Durmiente (Sleeping Beauty), an enormous glacier that lurks over the town. Living there is what it is like to live above the clouds.

It is also home to some of the most brutal living conditions on Earth. The town's fifty thousand residents spend much of the year in subzero temperatures. There is no running water, no sewage system, and no hospital. The government has no real presence in the town.

The town is only accessible by braving a dangerous mountainside road that is covered by grass, rocks, dirt, and often ice. The journey can take several days, and those who visit learn that there are no hotels to stay in. The air makes it very difficult for visitors to breathe. Gravity holds oxygen close to the earth's surface, so altitude sickness is felt at around ten thousand feet.

Why would anyone ever want to live in such a place? The answer is "Money." Much of the population is made up of Peruvians hoping to strike it rich. The economy is built on unregulated gold mines. Miners work for thirty days without payment but can lay claim to any gold they find on the thirty-first day.

Lack of sanitation and the mining operations mean that the ground is heavily contaminated with mercury. Because of this, many of the residents suffer from mercury poisoning, which affects the nervous system and causes itching, burning, and skin discoloration. It seems absurd that people would actually live in such a place.

La Rinconada is a clear example of the lengths people will go to in order to obtain wealth. The men travel thirty minutes every day to enter gold mines filled with hazardous gases, mercury, and cyanide—all in hopes of striking it rich. They adapt to these harsh conditions, along with the difficulty of simply breathing each day.

These residents have conformed to their environment. They are living in a place no one should ever live. However, Christians can also conform to their culture and live in ways they should never live.

First Timothy 6:9 says, *People who want to be rich fall into all sorts of temptations and traps.* Have you allowed your desire for money or anything else to cause you to conform to this world? It can happen slowly, and you may not even realize it. Before you know it, your lifestyle is not honoring to God.

Live to please Jesus and to expand His kingdom.

COURAGE TO CHANGE

I obeyed this vision from heaven.
— **ACTS 26:19**

I have lived about an hour down the road from Jamestown, Virginia, for many years now. Jamestown is located on the James River a few miles from Williamsburg. The James River flows for 340 miles across eastern Virginia, through Richmond, and into the Tidewater region.

In 1607, 104 Englishmen and boys arrived in North America to start a settlement. On May 13, they chose the location for their new home and named it Jamestown after their king, James I. Jamestown became the first permanent English settlement in North America.

More than four hundred years ago, these English pioneers crossed the Atlantic Ocean on three ships: the *Godspeed*, the *Discovery*, and the *Susan Constant*. It was a voyage that took incredible courage, and it was financed by men with a vision for the future.

The adventurers sailed uncharted seas and traveled thousands of miles to follow their vision of religious freedom. The amount of courage it took to attempt such an unbelievable undertaking is hard to calculate, but they had a grand vision of a land of freedom—and that vision greatly inspired them.

The settlers established their town in the first year of the Jamestown settlement. In the second year, they established a town council. In the third year, the council voted to build a road five miles into the wilderness. In the fourth year, though, the English almost impeached the town council for trying to build that road.

The people who once had a great vision to travel across a gigantic ocean could not now see five miles into the wilderness. The people who once looked into the future with boldness now looked into it with fear.

The same thing can happen to us. In Acts 26:19, when Paul was speaking to King Agrippa, he said, *I obeyed this vision from heaven.* God had chosen Paul to preach the gospel to the gentiles and to spread the gospel to the known world. Paul followed that vision with great courage and boldness.

We must act in faith, not in fear. It is easy to get comfortable, even in a bad situation. We can become resistant instead of open to the new things God may want to do. New ways can be threatening to familiar ways. It can be hard to accept change when we don't know what will happen.

Be open, be willing, and be excited about new opportunities God is bringing into your life.

CRACK THE CODE

There is nothing hidden that will not be found.
There is no secret that will not be well known.
—LUKE 8:17

Kryptos is a sculpture in a courtyard at the Central Intelligence Agency headquarters in Langley, Virginia. It holds an encrypted message that has not yet been fully deciphered. It has been more than thirty years since the tall scroll of copper with thousands of punched-through letters was unveiled.

Three of the four passages from the sculpture have been decrypted, but one passage remains a mystery even after three decades, and that is a source of curiosity, consternation, and delight for thousands of people around the globe.

The sculptor, Jim Sanborn, has been hounded for years by code-breaking enthusiasts. Twice—in 2010 and again in 2014—he has provided clues to help these folks solve the passages. He has offered a clue to help solve the last passage. It is the word "Northeast" at positions 26 through 34.

Sanborn devised the codes that he used for the passages with the help of Edward Scheidt, retired chairman of the CIA's cryptographic center. The passages follow a theme of concealment and discovery, each more difficult than the last.

Lots of people really want to solve this puzzle. After so much time has passed and with only one passage remaining, there is a great desire by many to finally crack the code. While many problems in this world are seemingly unsolvable, this is one that has a chance of being solved.

But humanity's biggest problem has already been solved. Luke 8:16–17 tells us, *No one lights a lamp and puts it under a bowl or under a bed. A lamp is always put on a lampstand, so that people who come into a house will see the light. There is nothing hidden that will not be found. There is no secret that will not be well known.*

The word in the Greek for "hidden" is *kryptos*, the same as the name of the sculpture. Hiding the message of the sculpture is the point, but the point of the gospel is that it is *not* hidden. There is no code to crack in understanding God's message to us. It is not meant to be hidden, but it is a light for all to see.

The gospel message is that God loves us, wants to forgive us, and desires a personal relationship with us. Jesus is the way. He lights the path to God. Through Jesus, we can know purpose and meaning in this life and can spend eternity with God in the afterlife. It is a message that is crystal clear and is easy for anyone to comprehend.

CURRENT AFFAIRS

How is it that you don't know how
to interpret this present time?
—JESUS (LUKE 12:56 NIV)

Many of the people Jesus spoke to were fishermen or farmers who were quite skilled in their knowledge of the weather. They knew that different weather patterns indicated that changes were coming. However, they did not detect the momentous changes that would be coming from the message Christ was bringing to everyone. I can't help but wonder if all these years later, the same thing is happening again.

There is a passage in the Bible in which Jesus rebukes the people for their failure to recognize the real issues at work in the world. It is found in Luke 12:54–56 (NIV): *When you see a cloud rising in the west, immediately you say, "It's going to rain," and it does. And when the south wind blows, you say, "It's going to be hot," and it is. Hypocrites! You know how to interpret the appearance of the earth and the sky. How is it that you don't know how to interpret this present time?*

There is nothing wrong with knowing what is going on with the weather. One of the pastors at our church has a real interest in the weather, but he also is very interested in what God is doing. How many are up-to-date on all kinds of current affairs? They know what is happening in Washington. They know what the president is proposing and what Congress is debating, but do they know what God is doing? Are they aware of the work God wants done?

Many people are quick to know how the winds of change may be blowing at their job, but what about how God's purposes are being accomplished in our world? Do they know what part God wants them to play in His plan? How many are very knowledgeable about the latest celebrity gossip yet are ignorant of what the Lord is doing right in their own community and church?

There is nothing inherently wrong with you having an interest in politics, the economy, public opinion, or even Hollywood—but only if that interest is secondary to your understanding of what God's Word has to say about your work, your relationships, and your spiritual life. If as much energy and thought were put into familiarity with God's work that are put into all our other interests, we might have a very different situation in our lives and in our culture today.

God is always at work in our world. He wants us to join with Him to establish His kingdom. Being sensitive to His leading in our lives and being aware of His will are what should matter most.

DIRECTION, NOT DRIFT

We must keep going in the direction that we are now headed.
—PHILIPPIANS 3:16

A couple went on a vacation to Hawaii. They decided to do some snorkeling at the beach near their hotel. They went out into the lagoon to observe the aquatic life in the coral reef. They were mesmerized by all they saw—the coral, the colors, the variety of fish.

At some point, the husband lifted his head out of the water, and what he saw shocked him. They had been caught in a riptide without even realizing it. Focused on looking downward into the water, they had never looked up. Once they did look up, they realized they had drifted more than a mile out to sea. The shoreline looked impossibly far away. Their hotel looked like a mere blip in the distance.

Fortunately, they had a body board with them. They grabbed it and began furiously paddling back to shore. They swam for more than an hour before finally reaching the beach and collapsing in the sand. They were so close to disaster on a day intended to be a relaxing time at the beach.

That is a crazy story, but too many people can experience this same kind of thing with their lives. They look back over their past and realize they are far away from where they thought they would be. Somehow they drifted.

How can you maintain clear direction and avoid drifting in your life? Philippians 3:16 says, *We must keep going in the direction that we are now headed.* If we are not moving toward the goal, we will drift. Did you drift last week, last month, or last year? You cannot go somewhere else unless you acknowledge where you are right now. Have you allowed your focus to wander and drift away from your life's direction?

Where are you with your health, family, finances, career, or spiritual life? Where do you want to be? If you don't know where you are going, you won't get anywhere—or you will end up somewhere you don't want to be. You end up drifting to a destination you would not have chosen.

Determine your direction today. Decide that drifting ends now. It will take self-discipline and hard work, but it can be done. You have not drifted so far away that you cannot get back on course.

DO SOMETHING NEW

And whenever the clay would not take the shape he wanted, he
would change his mind and form it into some other shape.
—JEREMIAH 18:4

I recently visited Alaska's capital of Juneau. I learned there is no
way to get to Juneau by car. The only way to reach the state's
capital is by air or ship. Almost half of Alaska's population lives in
Anchorage, but that is not the capital.

The only major highway in the state goes to Anchorage,
allowing people the easiest access, yet Alaskans have never changed
their capital to Anchorage. Why not? I don't know the answer, but
I think it has something to do with insanity.

Actually, the classic definition of insanity is to repeat the same
thing the same way and expect different results. It is amazing how
much this happens in the church and in our own lives. Time and
time again, we expect God to do something new while we keep
doing the same thing we have always done!

Jeremiah 18:4 says, *And whenever the clay would not take the
shape he wanted, he would change his mind and form it into some
other shape*—a new shape. Praying for God to work is great, and

believing God for growth is right—but there are times when it takes something new.

There was a time when our church experienced an unusual number of people with serious illnesses, so we had two special healing services. The services were powerful, but God wanted us to do more. I felt led to do something we had never done before.

We decided to change our Sunday services for one week. Instead of our normal services, we would have a prayer meeting. Our normal praise and worship would not happen, the usual media and music would not take place, and I would not preach a message.

The entire service focused on seven different areas for prayer. We read Bible verses that dealt specifically with prayer. We had different leaders share faith declarations that spoke of our belief in what God can do.

The services were very impacting. We experienced something different from what we had before. People who had never been to one of our many prayer meetings saw what it was like to pray together.

The response was overwhelmingly positive. I thought some people might be upset that we did not have a normal service, or that they would be unhappy that they didn't get to sing or hear a sermon, but that did not happen.

Is there something new you should do? Are you expecting different results, a better situation, or a new blessing while still doing what you have always done?

It is time to do something new.

Start today.

DON'T FORGET TO REMEMBER

Don't forget about your leaders who taught you God's message. Remember what kind of lives they lived and try to have faith like theirs.

—HEBREWS 13:7

Ecclesiastes 9:15 says, *But the city was saved by the wisdom of a poor person who was soon forgotten.* A powerful king surrounded a small village with his army and was ready to attack. Somehow (the Bible does not tell us how) this poor man had an idea to save the city, and it worked! But he was soon forgotten. How could the people forget the man who had saved their lives? It seems unconscionable, but it still happens today. In fact, I think it happens most in the Christian community.

I once wrote a book on leadership, and in one chapter I talked about the importance of honoring those who are worthy of honor. I believe that we don't honor others nearly enough, and I think the reason for this is that we have a faulty understanding of pride and humility. Somehow we think that honoring people will make them prideful. In actuality, being honored should be humbling. It should not puff people up, but it should foster gratitude. The people being honored should recognize the many people who helped them along the road to their accomplishments. They should be thankful, not egotistical.

Hebrews 13:7 tells us, *Don't forget about your leaders who taught you God's message. Remember what kind of lives they lived and try to have faith like theirs.* Don't forget to remember to honor those who are worthy of honor. *Tima*, the Greek word in the New Testament for "honor," means to value, respect, or reverence.

Honor is first an attitude, but it must become an act to be complete. There needs to be specific times when we honor those who have earned it—people such as parents, spouses, pastors, and leaders; people who have exhibited qualities like perseverance, faithfulness, and godliness; people who have had great successes and have accomplished much—people who have made a huge difference in the lives of so many others.

Too many times we wait far too long—or never—to honor someone. Usually it is at the end of someone's career or life. I was recently at a retirement banquet where honor was given. It was great to witness, but we should not wait until someone's retirement to honor them. Giving someone an award or rewarding them with a special gift is the right thing to do. Showing appreciation and highlighting work well done does not need to be delayed until someone's later years.

Look for ways to honor those who are worthy of it. Establish processes for honoring people. We will find much to honor if we intentionally observe. When you see people who have earned honor, don't forget to remember them.

THE ULTIMATE VACCINE

I will keep on being glad, because I know that your prayers and the help that comes from the Spirit of Christ Jesus will keep me safe.
—PHILIPPIANS 1:18–19

As I write this, we are in the midst of an unprecedented campaign to vaccinate Americans against the COVID-19 virus. However, it is not the first time there has been a vaccination campaign. In fact, it started more than two hundred years ago in a small town in Massachusetts. Highly contagious smallpox led to fevers and skin rashes that could leave permanent scars. Much worse was that 30 percent of cases were fatal.

In 1796, English physician Edward Jenner developed the first vaccine for smallpox, but there were doubts that an injection containing a virus found in sick cows (cowpox) could really protect humans from smallpox. It sounded too good to be true that a vaccine could stop the spread of the most devastating disease of the era.

In 1809 in Milton, Massachusetts, Dr. Amos Holbrook vaccinated twelve children who were then quarantined together and carefully observed for any sign of smallpox. Fifteen days later, the quarantine ended—and no child had contracted smallpox.

This bold experiment was the first municipal vaccination campaign in the United States, and it helped to remove some doubts about vaccination. News of the result of the vaccine was distributed to every town in Massachusetts. This led to an 1810 law that directed every municipality in the state to offer vaccinations.

Smallpox vaccinations became routine, and the practice spread all over the world. By 1980, smallpox had been eradicated, in part because of twelve young smallpox-vaccine pioneers. The handwritten card certifying the event lists the children's names, and the card is displayed in the National Museum of American History in Washington, DC.

Many are hopeful that the vaccine for COVID-19 will decrease sickness and save lives and may help us return to our regular way of life. However, the vaccine will only help with COVID-19—it does not keep us safe from any other disease.

In Philippians 1:18–19 Paul wrote, *I will keep on being glad, because I know that your prayers and the help that comes from the Spirit of Christ Jesus will keep me safe.* Even though Paul was in jail at the time, he knew that with the prayers of his friends, God would keep him safe.

The safety God provides is far greater than a single vaccine administered for a single disease. Through our faith in Christ, the Holy Spirit protects us from all manner of dangers—whether physical, spiritual, emotional, financial, or any other type of jeopardy.

It is good to know that God is always there to protect us and keep us safe. He is the ultimate vaccine. Ask for God's help for yourself and others, knowing He will keep you from harm.

FOLLOWING THE FOOTSTEPS

Some men joined him and believed, among them Dionysius the Areopagite, a woman named Damaris, and others with them.
—ACTS 17:34 (NKJV)

While I was in Athens, Greece, I had the opportunity to visit Mars Hill. It is in the area of the Acropolis. Unlike the Parthenon and other famous man-made structures, it is literally a big natural rocky area. I was struck by the idea that it has not changed much in almost two thousand years. Where I was standing was much like it was when Paul spoke there.

The apostle Paul visited Athens by himself when Silas and Timothy stayed behind in Berea. He toured the city and saw many idols. Paul was invited to speak at Mars Hill, the place where philosophers gathered to discuss ideas.

At the time, two philosophical schools were dominant. The Epicureans followed Epicurus, who taught that happiness and pleasure were the main goals of life. They believed that the gods were remote and uninvolved. The Stoics followed Zeno, who taught that people should learn self-control and be free of emotion. They were pantheistic, seeing everything as an expression of their gods.

They called Paul a "babbler." The word in the Greek is *spermologos*. *Logos* means "word," and *spermo* means "seed." The idea was that Paul picked up seeds of knowledge but had no developed system of thought. It was a major insult, especially to an intellectual like Paul. He had been taught at a great university and had then studied under a famous rabbi. He knew Stoic philosophy and was well read in literature.

Athens was the world center of culture, religion, and philosophy. Paul found a way to connect with Greece's scholars by mentioning their altar to an "Unknown God." Paul is a model for how to reach an unsaved, unchurched, post-Christian culture. Indeed, Greek culture at the time was much like ours today.

Our starting point for a conversation about Jesus might be something in the news, a movie, or a streaming show. We need to meet people where they are and follow in Paul's footsteps by connecting our interactions to the gospel. In his message, Paul also quoted from popular literature. He quoted from Minos's letter to his father, Zeus, and from the poet Epimenides.

Paul's ability to relate to the Greeks gained him a hearing to share the gospel. He started by talking about God as the creator and source of life. Paul made clear that God was not someone humans made up, nor could He be worshiped as an idol. He then presented Jesus and the resurrection.

Acts 17:34 (NKJV) says, *Some men joined him and believed, among them Dionysius the Areopagite, a woman named Damaris, and others with them.* When we make the gospel relatable to people, and when we talk in practical and relevant ways about following Jesus, people will respond!

FORGIVE ME THIS WRONG

How were you inferior to the other churches, except that
I was never a burden to you? Forgive me this wrong!
—2 CORINTHIANS 12:13 (NIV)

The apostle Paul wrote almost one-third of the New Testament.
In all that he wrote, he only apologized one time. The apology
is found in 2 Corinthians 12:13 (NIV), where he writes, *How were
you inferior to the other churches, except that I was never a burden
to you? Forgive me this wrong!* Why did Paul apologize? What did
he apologize for?

Paul was defending his ministry to the Corinthians, and he
apologized for not taking up any offerings from them. This is a
remarkable statement from Paul, and it challenges Christ followers
in a salient way. If the only time Paul ever apologized was for not
taking up offerings, then the importance of offerings in a local
church had been elevated to the highest level.

In the previous chapter of 2 Corinthians, Paul wrote, *Was it a sin
for me to lower myself in order to elevate you by preaching the gospel of
God to you free of charge? I robbed other churches by receiving support
from them so as to serve you* (2 Corinthians 11:7–8 NIV).

Paul received financial support from other churches so he could preach to the Corinthians for free. Upon further reflection, he determined he was wrong for having done so.

The Corinthians were not treated as inferior to any other church. The same gospel was preached and the same Spirit was at work. The only difference was that they did not financially support the ministry, and Paul had to have other churches give offerings so he could minister to them.

Paul's words may also contain some irony. The Corinthian believers were inferior only in the sense that Paul did not burden them financially—a wrong for which he now asked to be forgiven.

Irony or not, what is clear is that Paul realized that the Corinthians should have supported their church with offerings. His desire to focus on people more than offerings reflects his pastoral heart. His commitment to establish and grow the church is certainly correct, but at some point he realized that the people had taken his generosity for granted.

There is no ownership by the people of a church when they do not give. The responsibility to meet the needs of the church falls on its members and attenders. By taking an offering, everyone is given the opportunity to support God's work. By giving, the people show their obedience to God and their support for the church— and there should never be an apology for that.

YOUR ADVISORY TEAM

Without wise leadership, a nation falls;
there is safety in having many advisers.
—PROVERBS 11:14 (NLT)

I f you are going to make wise decisions, and if you are going to make great decisions, you will require assistance. We all need counsel and advice in order to make certain decisions and to make them well.

Life is very complex. It is challenging. Modern life is the most complex that the world has ever seen. There were times in history when life was simpler and when there were fewer choices, but today there are so many options.

You can't decide anything without having a multitude of options and choices. Even when trying to buy an electronic device or an appliance, you can be faced with ten different varieties and multiple brands. Almost every decision requires a great amount of wisdom to make the right call.

Also, we live in a culture in which many people are giving advice. Bloggers, talk-show hosts, and celebrities all give out a lot of advice; whether they are qualified or correct in their advice is another issue.

That is why you need to form an advisory team—a group of people who have your back and can give you wise advice. You need to intentionally think about forming a team of people who can be your advisers. As Proverbs 11:14 (NLT) says, *Without wise leadership, a nation falls; there is safety in having many advisers.*

We started out in life with an advisory team. We began with a preordained team of advisers made up of our parents, teachers, and coaches. When we are young, we don't choose our advisers. They choose us, and they are there to give us advice that helps us in the early days of our lives so that we start out in the right direction.

Particularly when we reach young adulthood, we have less and less contact with our childhood advisers. That is why it is so important to form an advisory team of people who can help us with decisions. There should be different kinds of people who have had different kinds of experiences, both negative and positive. They may be consultants, trainers, financial advisers, pastors, or various friends.

Ultimately, you've got to make the call for your own life, but it is good to hear different perspectives and opinions. It is good to know how wise people see an issue.

You have to personally know the people who are on your team. When you listen to their advice and act on it, the results can be marvelous. The advice that they give you could spare you from heartache, keep you from the negative consequences of a bad decision, or lead you into a really good situation.

Ideally, we make marvelous decisions because we receive the kind of perspective and input we need. Take the time today to make a short list of trusted people for your advisory team.

LEAVE YOUR PAST BEHIND

Anyone who belongs to Christ is a new person.
The past is forgotten, and everything is new.
—2 CORINTHIANS 5:17

Leap year occurs once every four years. Of course, that is when we add a day to the calendar at the end of February so that we are correctly aligned with the earth's rotation around the sun. One year is actually about 365.25 days long, so adding an extra day every four years is necessary to keep our calendars accurate.

Six hours may not seem to be such a big deal, but after ten years without this extra day, the calendar would be off by two and a half days. After a century, the calendar would be off by a whopping twenty-five days! Over time, the natural seasons would literally occur in a totally different month on the out-of-whack calendar. Imagine summer in the U.S. in November!

Before the modern Gregorian calendar, people used the 365-day Julian calendar created by Roman emperor Julius Caesar in 46 BC. He included a leap year every four years, but his math wasn't quite right—there were eleven extra minutes per year. This gradually shifted the calendar off course.

In 1582, Pope Gregory XIII's astronomers identified the error and implemented the calendar and the leap-year system we use today. But since the calendar was off by eleven minutes a year for more than sixteen hundred years, something had to be done to correct it.

The pope decided that in order to bring the calendar up to date, ten days would have to be removed from it. Therefore, October 4, 1582, was followed by October 15, 1582. Ten days were removed from history forever! Whatever happened during those ten days is not part of the historical record. It is like a chronological mulligan!

It is remarkable to think that there are ten days in history that never happened. Imagine if you could choose ten days in your past and remove them from history—ten days where your foolish decisions, immoral actions, and hurtful words never even happened.

Second Corinthians 5:17 says, *Anyone who belongs to Christ is a new person. The past is forgotten, and everything is new.* When we confess our sins and accept Christ into our lives, God forgives us and forgets our past. He gives us a fresh start, a do-over, a new beginning.

We are justified, meaning we are "not guilty" in God's eyes. We have been acquitted; our record is clean. We can let go of our past regrets and refuse to dwell on them anymore. They are removed from our history, and God forgets that they ever happened.

Hanging on to the past keeps us from enjoying God's blessings today and blinds us to our future. Move forward and leave the past behind.

AGE IS AN ATTITUDE

I'm just as strong today as I was then [45 years ago],
and I can still fight as well in battle.
—JOSHUA 14:11

In 2021, Tom Brady won another Super Bowl, his record-breaking seventh, at the age of forty-three. In addition to that, he became the NFL MVP for the fifth time. It would be easy to call Brady's success an anomaly, but there is more to the story than that.

Like many other pioneers of the past, including Jackie Robinson, Jim Ryan, Tiger Woods, and so many more, Tom Brady has shown us what is possible. Instead of marveling at what Brady has done, though, let's think about what his success means for us.

Medical experts tell us there is a difference between chronological and biological age. Brady is a primary example. Tom House, Brady's personal throwing coach, has said that Tom is chronologically forty-three years old but biologically thirty-five. This explains his present success.

Brady is famous for his "TB12" method. He has even written a book about it. He follows a strict diet and exercise regimen that allows him to have a younger biological age.

Chronological age is the number of years a person has been alive, while biological age refers to how old a person seems. Biological age takes many lifestyle factors into consideration, including diet, exercise, stress, and sleeping habits, to name a few. Your biological age depends on these variables and can change on a continuing basis.

But age is an attitude and not just a number—even a biological one. We live in a youth-oriented culture, and after a lifetime of exposure to ageist language and negative attitudes, our thoughts about aging can become directed inward.

The list of ageist sentiments embedded in our everyday language is extensive. Aging is commonly equated with cognitive impairment and memory loss ("a senior moment") or an inability to learn new things ("You can't teach an old dog new tricks"). Ageist language also includes the use of the word "old" to describe something undesirable ("I'm not old. I'm just more mature").

This might lead us to think that we are too old to pursue new dreams. However, whether it's your career, a new relationship, or your connection with God, there is time for you to act. It is not too late. It can happen. It can be done.

We need the attitude of eighty-five-year-old Caleb. In Joshua 14:11, he says, *I am just as strong today as I was then [45 years ago], and I can still fight as well in battle.* Caleb wanted the land God had promised him, and his age was not going to stop him.

Shake things up, change course, and go in a new direction. Don't let your age keep you from pursuing what you are passionate about. Go for what God has for you!

GOD DIRECTS OUR STEPS

The LORD directs the steps of the godly.
He delights in every detail of their lives.
—**PSALM 37:23 (NLT)**

Psalm 37:23 (NLT) says, *The LORD directs the steps of the godly. He delights in every detail of their lives.* This single verse tells us so much about who God is and how He works in our lives. God cares about every detail of our lives—not just the big stuff, but all the stuff. He directs *every* step we take, not just some of them.

I recently talked with the wife of a pastor friend and discovered that we were born in the same city. She then showed me a postcard she had found in an antique store that had a picture of the hospital in which she had been born. I texted a picture of it to my dad to see if it was the same hospital where I was born—and it was!

What was remarkable was how all of this was revealed. I was not searching for it, yet it was made known to me. It was a blessing for me to see for the first time a picture of the place where I was born.

A couple of years ago, I was in New York City for some meetings, and my wife had come with me on the trip. We had some free time one afternoon, so we decided to visit the One World Trade Center.

We wanted to go to the observatory on the top of the building. We have been to New York City many times and have seen just about everything there is to see, but One WTC was new and provided an incredible view of the city.

After we left the building, I saw someone who looked just like my cousin Joy. She lives in Atlanta and I don't see her very often, but then I saw her husband, Don, and I knew it had to be them. I grabbed my wife, and we raced up to them. They were completely surprised. How is it that in a city of millions, we would run into each other at exactly that moment in time? I mean, what are the odds?

It would be hard to explain these events—and many more like them—if we did not know that God directs our steps. It would be hard to understand the value of these events unless we knew that God delights in every detail of our lives. The reality is that there are no coincidences with God; there is no such thing as luck. God directs our lives and delights in them.

God is at work. He guides us, blesses us, and gives us His favor. He delights in every detail of our lives, so let's live godly lives and enjoy these marvelous benefits.

GOD GIVES SECOND CHANCES

Mark can be very helpful to me,
so please find him and bring him with you.
—2 TIMOTHY 4:11

Dwayne Fields's prized moped was stolen one day. When he searched his London neighborhood, he found about ten guys dismantling it. He grabbed the moped, and a fight broke out. One guy shot at Fields at point-blank range and then pulled the trigger and shot again. Dwayne ran away looking for bullet wounds and blood. Amazingly, he had not been hit. He had been given a second chance at life. In fact, the experience so changed Fields that he went on to become the first black Briton to walk to the North Pole.

The gospel is all about second chances. Most importantly, it is about God's forgiveness of our sins. Sometimes it is hard for people to believe they can be forgiven. People need to know that God does not give up on us simply because we mess up. God is willing to give us another opportunity to get it right, even after we may completely fail.

The Bible is replete with examples of second chances. Moses received the Ten Commandments from God. When he returned to the camp and came upon a huge hedonistic party, he was so angry that he threw down the tablets, destroying them. Fortunately, God gave him another copy. This is the same Moses who in anger killed an Egyptian who was abusing a Hebrew. God gave Moses a second chance, and he ended up becoming one of the world's all-time greatest leaders.

Peter was one of Jesus' disciples, and yet when Jesus was unjustly arrested, Peter denied that he ever knew Him. He did not just deny Him once, but he denied Him three different times. Peter felt like such a failure that he went back to his former profession as a fisherman. However, Jesus went to him and gave him a second chance. He gave Peter the opportunity to serve Him and help lead the early church.

Mark was an early follower of Jesus, and he wrote the gospel of Mark. He was on the ministry team of the apostle Paul. The book of Acts tells us that he deserted Paul and the team, left Perga, and went back to Jerusalem. Ten years later, Paul was imprisoned in Rome. In 2 Timothy 4:11, Paul wrote, *Mark can be very helpful to me, so please find him and bring him with you.* Even after deserting him, Paul gave Mark a second chance.

God gave Moses a second chance, Jesus gave Peter a second chance, and Paul gave Mark a second chance. Offering forgiveness and giving second chances are what Jesus and His followers do.

GOD NEVER WASTES ANYTHING

New wine must be put into new wineskins.
Both the skins and the wine will then be safe.
—MATTHEW 9:17

After years of drought, in 2019 there was record-breaking rain and snowfall in California. The rain for which many people had prayed finally came. Unfortunately, not a single major reservoir had been built in nearly forty years. California has a half-century-old master plan detailing dozens of new reservoirs to be built, yet none have been constructed. There was nowhere to store all the runoff that could have kept the state drought-free for years to come.

More than twenty million acre-feet of water was released into the sea. When the snowpacks melted, even more water was released and totally wasted. It is almost inconceivable that after suffering through one of the worst droughts in its history, California was completely unprepared to store this incredible blessing of record rain and snow. It is tragic to realize that all that precious water was simply wasted.

I couldn't help but think of Matthew 9:17, where Jesus said, *No one pours new wine into old wineskins. The wine would swell and burst the old skins. Then the wine would be lost, and the skins would be ruined. New wine must be put into new wineskins. Both the skins and the wine will then be safe.* The message of Jesus was simply that the new wine of the gospel called for new wineskins to hold it. The good news would bring abundant and eternal life to spiritually empty people who could then receive it.

Because Jesus' words are as relevant today as when He spoke them, the gospel is still being proclaimed and people who seek Him can still receive forgiveness and eternal life. If anyone is open and will let go of previous ideas, traditions, and beliefs, they can receive Jesus. God will only bring something new into our lives if we are ready to receive it. As long as we hold on to old models, old behaviors, and old structures, God cannot pour in the new wine.

Sometimes Christ followers get upset with God because they do not believe they are receiving blessings like they should. However, God will not pour a blessing into a vessel that is not big enough to hold it.

God will not waste anything. He will not increase your influence if you are not ready to steward that influence. You must grow and change so God can pour blessings into your life that you can receive. You must develop in maturity so God can expand your influence.

Expand your reservoir so God can pour blessings in—and may less and less of His spiritual "rain" in your life get washed out to sea!

GOD'S GROWTH PLAN

I am the true vine, and my Father is the gardener.
—JOHN 15:1

A while ago my wife decided that she wanted to plant some rose bushes in front of our house. She told me there was a kind that needed very little attention yet bloomed with beautiful roses. They are called "Knock Out Roses." These bushes have continuous blooms, compact growth, and are very hardy—especially for flowers.

They are popular because they are the first no-maintenance rose—perfect for the lazy or inexperienced gardener. You hardly have to water, spray, or fertilize them. You just plant them and they will bloom, bloom, bloom with no work or care.

So we planted them, and sure enough, they produced beautiful red roses and made the front of our house look nice. Last fall, our landscapers cut them way down. They pruned the bushes to about a third of their height. I was surprised since they did not do that the previous year. I wondered what the roses would look like this spring.

Well, the bushes are back to their large, healthy size, and the roses are once again blooming beautifully, just like last year.

As I admired the roses, I couldn't help but think of the words of Jesus in John 15:1–2: *I am the true vine, and my Father is the gardener. He cuts away every branch of mine that doesn't produce fruit. But he trims clean every branch that does produce fruit, so that it will produce even more fruit.*

God's way of producing growth is to prune us. Pruning does not look or feel good. Going backward to go forward is not something most of us would sign up for in life, yet Jesus tells us that God will cut away what He thinks is holding us back from attaining greater growth.

It turns out there was a reason the landscapers pruned our rose bushes. The Knock Out Rose has a weakness: rose rosette, a virus first discovered in the western United States around 1940. The virus is spread by eriophyid mites, which are so tiny that they literally blow into gardens on the wind. When the mites feed on a rose, they transmit the virus.

Because a virus causes rose rosette, it eventually spreads internally to every part of the plant. The only sure way to keep from having rose rosette is to prune back the bushes by two-thirds while they're dormant to remove any overwintering mites and eggs in the bud crevices.

Sometimes God prunes us. He cuts away the spiritual viruses that might otherwise destroy us. He also trims away what may be working so He can bring something even better into our lives. If you are walking with God but feel diminished right now, know that in the next season, you will bloom beautifully.

GOD'S MESSAGE IN THE PANDEMIC

Paul and his friends went through Phrygia and Galatia,
but the Holy Spirit would not let them preach in Asia.
—ACTS 16:6

The pandemic was a gigantic disruption to our lives. Everything from work, school, recreation, and even church was impacted. But it is not the first time plans have changed.

The apostle Paul took the gospel to the known world. He wanted to continue expanding the church into Asia, but God stopped him. He did not allow Paul to preach the gospel in certain regions, and He actually stopped Paul twice.

Acts 16:6–7 tells us, *Paul and his friends went through Phrygia and Galatia, but the Holy Spirit would not let them preach in Asia. After they arrived in Mysia, they tried to go into Bithynia, but the Spirit of Jesus would not let them.*

What a remarkable event! Throughout the New Testament, Christ followers are told to preach the gospel, to share the good news. Yet here God stops them—just like the church was stopped from in-person, regular meetings for much of the pandemic.

Could God do His greatest work in the new reality of a broken plan? Since God has a purpose for all of us, then He must have been up to something. The virus certainly did not take Him by surprise. Was there something new we needed to discover?

Paul ended up going to Macedonia, and it changed history. Christianity advanced from Asia Minor to Europe. The church was established in Europe and then spread throughout the world. Now there are more than two-and-a-half-billion Christians worldwide. It never would have happened without God's disruption.

Paul responded enthusiastically and positively to the change in his plans. He could have been mad at God or felt sorry for himself. He could have begrudgingly gone to Europe without giving himself to the work. Instead, he established the church in many cities.

We are like Paul in a situation we did not plan to be in. No one could have ever predicted that Christians would be stopped from meeting on Sundays for services. It is a total disruption—a complete change from everything we normally do.

Paul went to Macedonia because he had a dream of a man asking him to come over and help them. In the midst of this change to our lives and churches, there is an opportunity to do even greater good and to have a greater impact.

The church is not stopped, and it is certainly not defeated. We have a new chance and a new possibility. Jesus went to Calvary, and all seemed lost—but He triumphed over death and won the victory.

We can do so too.

EVEN IN BARREN PLACES

The LORD asked Abraham, "Why did Sarah laugh? Does she doubt that she can have a child in her old age?"
—**GENESIS 18:13**

I have always wanted to visit Volcanoes National Park in Hawaii. I think volcanoes are fascinating. They exist all over our planet, and no one knows when they will erupt. At Volcanoes National Park, you get to see several volcanoes and the damage their eruptions have caused.

I finally had the opportunity to visit. I was so excited that we actually arrived before the visitor center opened. I talked with a park ranger, and she confirmed my plan for the day. She encouraged us to take our hike on the Kīlauea Iki Trail first before the parking lot filled up and there were too many hikers on the trail.

The four-mile trail descends four hundred feet through a lush rain forest to the floor of the solidified Kīlauea Iki Crater lava lake. You can walk all the way across the still-steaming crater floor. Along the way, you can peer into the vent below the Puʻu Puaʻi cinder cone, which in 1959 erupted to a height of nineteen hundred feet. Then you return on the other side to the crater's rim.

It was a great hike down to the caldera floor. As we walked across the hardened lava, I saw something quite unusual: a small tree was growing through a crack in the crater floor. How could anything possibly grow in such a hostile environment? It was shocking to see leaves and even some flowers on a tree rooted in such total barrenness.

To be barren was considered a curse in the ancient world. In fact, it was even grounds for divorce. Genesis 18:13 says, *The Lord asked Abraham, "Why did Sarah laugh? Does she doubt that she can have a child in her old age?"* Sarah laughed at the thought of having a child at her advanced age, but God miraculously gave her Isaac.

Several other women in the Bible were barren: Rebekah, Rachel, Hannah, and Elizabeth. All of those women eventually gave birth. Their sons are some of the greatest men to have ever lived: Jacob, Joseph, Samuel, and John the Baptist.

The reality is that God can do something new in any situation, including in abject barrenness. He can bring life when there appears to be no hope. God can create growth in all kinds of environments.

If you find yourself in a barren place, just know that God has not abandoned you. There may be a time of waiting, but don't believe that nothing can be birthed or grow in barrenness—because it positively can.

HEALTHY TRANSITIONS

There is a time for everything,
and a season for every activity under the heavens.
—ECCLESIASTES 3:1 (NIV)

'll never forget when our oldest son, Matt, left home for college. It was an experience that was different from anything our family had ever gone through before. It was the kind of experience that changed us all.

It was also a natural and appropriate transition for our family. There was nothing wrong with it. There was nothing unhealthy about it. It was exactly what should have happened. Matt was leaving to begin his independent life and earn a degree for his future career.

However, it was still a very challenging experience. It challenged me as a father, it challenged my wife as a mother, and it challenged his brother, Wes. It brought a lot of tears, and it caused us to have to restructure the way we did things in our family.

Transitions can be extremely challenging, yet at the same time they can be absolutely normal and beneficial. The one thing they will not be is uneventful. They will always bring changes into your life.

As Ecclesiastes 3:1 (NIV) says, *There is a time for everything, and a season for every activity under the heavens.* I like to compare spiritual seasons to the natural seasons. Just as there is a transition between every natural season, so there is also a transition between every spiritual season.

Although seasons of transition visit us all, they don't happen in the same way or in the same order. There are times in our lives when we will move between seasons very quickly, but there are other times when we will be in a rather lengthy season of transition.

It is also important to point out that there is a distinct difference between transition and change. I think of change as primarily, though not exclusively, external (finding a new doctor, moving across town, etc.). Transition is primarily, though not exclusively, internal (deciding to get married, letting go of a past trauma, etc.). That is why transition generates so much more emotion than other changes in life. Transition is the process you go through to come to terms with the new season God brings to your life.

However, it can be challenging. It can be a time when we are not clear about exactly what is going on. It can be a time when we may wonder what God is up to, but during transitions, God is still at work. He is at work in a way that takes us from one season to another.

Welcome transition into your life. Embrace it as God's way of bringing you out of one season and into a new one.

HEARING FROM GOD

Now at last, God sent his Son to bring his message to us.
—HEBREWS 1:2

People have been seeking God and His guidance for many centuries. About twenty-five hundred years ago, Delphi, Greece, was considered the place where heaven and Earth met. It was believed to be the place on Earth in closest proximity to the gods. The city was dedicated to the worship of Zeus's son, who supposedly lived there.

Delphi was known for its oracle residing at the temple of Apollo. It was believed that Apollo spoke through the oracle, offering wisdom on everything from public policy to personal affairs. The oracle of Delphi was famous throughout the world. People would visit from all across Greece, as well as from places such as Egypt, Rome, and Turkey.

In many ways, Delphi was considered the center of the known world. When anyone from a peasant to a king needed wisdom, Delphi was the place to go. Whenever guidance was needed about whether to go to war or whether to get married, the oracle was consulted. People came to get a word from God (or more accurately, the gods).

The methods used were very strange. Apollo would speak through a virgin who was more than forty years old and who was in a drug-induced state. If an animal froze when it had cold water dumped on it, then the oracle could not seek direction that day; but if the animal shook off the water, then it could be sacrificed. If eagles flew in a certain direction, then that was your guidance. If the wind made a certain sound or blew in a certain way through the oak trees, therein was your answer.

It is remarkable how long people have sought to know God's will. For thousands of years, people have sought His guidance and direction in their lives—to know what they are to do with their lives. Hebrews 1:1–2 says, *Long ago in many ways and at many times God's prophets spoke his message to our ancestors. But now at last, God sent his Son to bring his message to us.*

Today we are so blessed that we can have God speak directly to us. We do not need to look to oracles, eagles, or oak trees. We do not need to travel to a faraway place to hear from Him. We do not need to engage in bizarre practices to receive guidance.

He guides us through His Word, the Bible. We can receive such guidance for our lives by reading it. We are also blessed that we have the Holy Spirit. The Spirit guides us into God's will for our lives. The Word and the Spirit are all we need in order to hear from God!

IN THE CITY

He is not here; he has risen, just as he said.
Come and see the place where he lay.
—**MATTHEW 28:6** (NIV)

I have been fortunate to have been able to visit some of the greatest cities in the world, but only one of them is *the City*. There can be only one Jerusalem.

During my visit to the Holy Land, I saw and experienced many marvelous sites, yet my greatest desire during the trip was to go to the Holy City. There is no city in the ancient or modern world throughout history that has captivated humanity more than Jerusalem.

Jerusalem is both an ancient and a modern city. The modern areas of Jerusalem are similar to many other major cities, but to visit the ancient city is something entirely different. To see it from the Mount of Olives is quite a sight and captures the totality of the ancient city.

There is nothing like walking through the Jaffa Gate to actually enter Jerusalem. It is mindboggling to realize all who have entered this city throughout history—it is a "who's who" of religious leadership.

As we walked through ancient Jerusalem, I was enamored by much of what I saw, but I was waiting for the ultimate site. My excitement built as we approached the Church of the Holy Sepulchre, built on the site where some believe Jesus was crucified, buried, and rose again. It was the middle of the afternoon on a Tuesday, and the place was packed with people.

Those who question the impact or future of Christianity would never have doubted it that day. The numbers of people simply added to the experience for me.

Our first stop was at the rock of Calvary, the place where Jesus was unjustly and mercilessly murdered. It is a poignant moment to actually stand near where your Savior died for you—not just in a spiritual sense, but in the literal physical space.

From there we went to a tomb/cave much like the one Jesus was buried in. It may not have been the actual tomb, but seeing it was an experience unlike any other. It was a special experience to peer inside and realize that a small cave like this was where Jesus was buried and rose again.

I read Matthew 28:5–6 (NIV): *Do not be afraid, for I know that you are looking for Jesus, who was crucified. He is not here; he has risen, just as he said. Come and see the place where he lay.*

I have been a follower of Christ, a pastor, and a Christian leader for a long time, but being in that place was the spiritual highlight of my life. The resurrection never seemed more real to me than on that day. I hope someday you have the opportunity to visit and experience it too.

ACCEPTING THE UNACCEPTABLE

Father, if you are willing, take this cup from me;
yet not my will, but yours be done.
—LUKE 22:42 (NIV)

On the last day of my trip to the Holy Land, we went to the Mount of Olives. It was there Jesus took His disciples to the garden of Gethsemane to pray. He knew He was going to be arrested that very night, and He wanted the support of the disciples in His greatest moment of need.

Luke recorded the prayer Jesus prayed that forever changed human history: *Father, if you are willing, take this cup from me; yet not my will, but yours be done* (Luke 22:42 NIV).

Jesus did the will of the Father—not His own will—when He went to the cross and died for our sins. Because He did, every human being has the opportunity for a relationship with God and eternal life.

Standing on the Mount of Olives, Jesus would have looked down upon Jerusalem. As I stood there in the same place, I realized how close Jesus was to Jerusalem—but also how close He was to escape. All Jesus had to do was walk up the mountain and down the other side, and He would have been in Bethany—a hike that would have taken Him only an hour.

Jesus did not have to go to the cross. He had an easy and quick way to escape the pain and suffering that awaited Him. However, He chose to accept God's will rather than do His own will. He chose to accept the unacceptable.

It is never easy to accept the unacceptable in your life. Accepting what you cannot change is the pathway to peace—but it eludes many. We cannot change the weather, we cannot change the past, and we positively cannot change another person against their will.

Years ago, I went through an experience in which I just could not accept what was happening to me. It was unfair and I was being wronged, but there was nothing I could do to change it. Finally, after weeks of misery (and making my family miserable), I asked God to help me accept the situation. Absolutely nothing changed except me. I received peace by accepting what I could not change.

Jesus accepted God's plan, even though He did not want to walk the path of suffering. He chose acceptance, and that freed Him to fulfill God's will.

We must determine that either God has a plan for us or He does not; either God is for us or He is not; either God has our best interests in mind or He does not. Accepting God's will is sometimes so difficult that we just cannot do it in our own power.

As we surrender our will to His, He will make a way for us. In fact, accepting His will means walking into our destiny—not away from it.

JESUS THE HEALER

Jesus felt sorry for the man. So he put his hand on him and said,
"I want to! Now you are well."

—MARK 1:41

Healing for physical and emotional sickness is part of God's plan for our lives. Jesus is the Great Physician who healed people throughout His ministry, and He continues to do so today. He cares about your body and mind just as much as your soul. In the kingdom of God, healing is the default mode for health.

There may be doubt in our minds whether or not Jesus wants us to be healed, but consider Mark 1:40–42: *A man with leprosy came to Jesus and knelt down. He begged, "You have the power to make me well, if only you wanted to." Jesus felt sorry for the man. So he put his hand on him and said, "I want to! Now you are well." At once the man's leprosy disappeared, and he was well.*

Jesus wants to heal you!

We do not discourage a sick friend from going to the doctor, yet we can be wary of encouraging him to pursue divine healing. The Bible is full of stories of people being healed. The stories are very diverse in the way someone is healed, who facilitates the healing, and the process of the healing, but one factor in Scripture is always the same: people get healed of their sicknesses.

The most practical book in the Bible is James. We can read there about how to gain wisdom, how to deal with conflict, and how to communicate effectively. James 5:14–15 even tells us how to be healed: *If you are sick, ask the church leaders to come and pray for you. Ask them to put olive oil on you in the name of the Lord. If you have faith when you pray for sick people, they will get well. The Lord will heal them.*

That is pretty straightforward. Ask to be healed, believe you will be healed, and then thank God for your healing. If you are sick or have an illness, you want to be healed. If you have been diagnosed with a disease, you need God's healing touch. If someone you care about needs to be healed, you want to do whatever you can to help them.

We need miracle-working faith that believes that God is eager to heal. Activating and increasing our faith is what we need to do. Faith is not just something we cling to in tough times, but it is also something we cultivate for greater spiritual power.

God values faith and responds to it. Let your faith be active rather than passive, immediate rather than eventual, and spiritual rather than mental—and then see the healing work that God can do.

LOVE IN ACTION

Let us not love with words or speech but with actions and in truth.
—1 JOHN 3:18 (NIV)

Valentine's Day is a day when we focus on love. It is usually about romantic love. Couples go out to dinner, give each other gifts, and do other intimate things. It is a great way to celebrate your love.

I have enjoyed many Valentine's Days with my wife, Michelle. We have celebrated in both small and big ways. Sometimes we have celebrated with a special gift or trip, and other times with more simple festivities. Last year we had a delicious dinner by the ocean on a warm February night.

Love is not only reserved for romance—or for Valentine's Day. First John 3:17–18 (NIV) says, *If anyone has material possessions and sees a brother or sister in need but has no pity on them, how can the love of God be in that person? Dear children, let us not love with words or speech but with actions and in truth.*

I was recently in the Dominican Republic. It was not for a vacation in Punta Cana, but I was there for ministry. I visited a small village as well as the city of Santo Domingo. I witnessed extreme poverty in both places. Whether I was in a rural village or the inner city, I observed great material need.

I was also fortunate enough to meet a five-year-old boy named Sael. I call him by his middle name, Daniel. He is the child my wife and I sponsor through Compassion International. I was also able to meet his mother and little sister and to visit their very modest home. It was about the size of the living room in my house. Their home consisted of a tiny kitchen, a small bedroom, and a little family room. This family needs all the help we can give them.

It is heartbreaking to see such a situation. It can certainly leave you with gratitude for how God has blessed you, but love requires more than just having your heart touched or being filled with gratitude. Love is not just about feelings or words; love requires action.

We must show God's love in practical ways. For Daniel, love is when others give monthly so he can be taught and cared for by his church. Other children might see love when someone mentors them or buys them school supplies. Homeless veterans might recognize love when someone feeds them. Still other people might recognize love when people donate food or clothes to meet their basic needs.

God wants us to show His love by our actions, not just by our words. When we do so, God is pleased and the world takes notice.

MAKING A COMMITMENT

Commit everything you do to the Lord. Trust him to help you
do it, and he will.
—**PSALM 37:5** (TLB)

I remember when my eldest son was commissioned as an officer in
the army. He raised his right hand and repeated these words: "I, Matt
McDaniel, swear that I will support and defend the Constitution of
the United States against all enemies, foreign and domestic; that I will
bear true faith and allegiance to the same; that I take this obligation
freely, without any mental reservations or purpose of evasion; and
that I will well and faithfully discharge the duties of the office upon
which I am about to enter. So help me God."

It is a big commitment to commit to put your life in harm's
way, but we all need to make commitments. "I pledge allegiance,"
"To tell the whole truth," and "I do" are some of the common
ones. In truth, you can't live without making commitments.
The person who refuses to make commitments will be a person
without God, without a job, and possibly without a home or
many other things in life. There is certainly no way to make an
impact without commitment.

The willingness to make commitments is a mark of maturity—both emotional and spiritual. Only an immature person tries to slide through life without committing to anything. In fact, it is the fear of commitment that causes many to miss God's blessings.

Think about any significant relationship in your life, whether marriage, friendship, parenting, or work. The strength of any given relationship is measured by our commitment. Can people count on us? If we are not committed, our relationships will be unreliable, and thus unfulfilling.

Keeping a commitment can sometimes be very costly, but the cost of not following through can be even more expensive. Trying to get out of our commitments will cost us our relationships, our success, and ultimately everything of real and lasting value.

There is a tremendous power in commitment. Commitment always unlocks the door to opportunities, to potential, to spiritual growth, and to miracles. Successful people are just ordinary people who have chosen to make commitments that others are unwilling to make.

During my many years as a Christian, I have watched God miraculously enable me to fulfill commitments that I made in faith—even if I had no idea ahead of time how I was going to fulfill them! God always makes a way when we fully trust Him. Consider and meditate on the powerful words of Psalm 37:5 (TLB): *Commit everything you do to the Lord. Trust him to help you do it, and he will.*

MASSIVE MIRACLE

The sea opened up, and the Israelites walked through on dry land with a wall of water on each side.
—**EXODUS 14:21–22**

The crossing of the Red Sea was a massive miracle. Exodus 12:37–38 tells us, *There were about six hundred thousand of them, not counting women and children. Many other people went with them as well, and there were also a lot of sheep, goats, and cattle.* Scholars believe the total number of people was close to 2.5 million men, women, and children, in addition to the animals.

A quartermaster general in the U.S. Army did an evaluation to determine what would be needed to care for such a huge number of people. He determined that three million pounds of food and eleven million gallons of water would be needed every day. The camp would need to be two-thirds the size of Rhode Island in order to have room to pitch the tents and pen the animals.

The people of Israel were trapped between the Red Sea and the Egyptian army. Exodus 14:21–22 tells us, *The LORD sent a strong east wind that blew all night until there was dry land where the water had been. The sea opened up, and the Israelites walked through on dry land with a wall of water on each side.*

The quartermaster general reported that it would take thirty-five days to cross double file on a narrow path through the Red Sea, but the Israelites crossed the Red Sea in one day. In order for everyone to walk across in one day, the path would have had to have been at least three miles wide with people walking five thousand abreast.

The massiveness of this miracle is hard to fathom. Food and water were needed every day for a population the size of Houston, Texas. Understanding the logistics of this miracle should cause us to consider just how great our God really is. As we face illness, disease, financial shortfalls, relational problems, or whatever else may challenge us, we can know that these problems are not too big for our God.

Our initial response may be one of wonder and amazement, but we must move past that to a place of active faith. God may not work in a way we want or expect, but He will act. He is at work, and His purposes will be accomplished regardless of present circumstances.

God is never caught off guard, and He has a bigger plan than we can see. Our responsibility is to believe—to put our faith in an all-powerful God who does impossible things. The same God who parted the Red Sea is the same God who can do a miracle in your life.

MORE PRECIOUS THAN GOLD

These trials will show that your faith is genuine. It is being tested as fire tests and purifies gold—though your faith is far more precious than mere gold.
1 PETER 1:7 (NLT)

Gold has enamored humankind for centuries. The search for it has led people to travel great distances, make enormous sacrifices, and risk their very lives. The gold rush in California resulted in so many people going there that it accelerated California's road to statehood. The NFL's San Francisco 49ers are named after that famed gold rush that began at Sutter's Mill near Sacramento in 1849.

About fifty years later, Felix Pedro, an immigrant from Italy, discovered gold in Alaska. Pedro had spent years in Alaska searching for gold, but when he actually found it, he ran out of food. With no other option, Pedro had to leave his claim to get supplies. Upon his return, however, he could not find the spot where he had found the gold.

He continued to search for gold in the creeks and valleys of the Tanana Valley northeast of Fairbanks. On July 22, 1902, in a small stream (now called Pedro Creek), he discovered gold. Pedro's now-famous words about the discovery were, "There's gold in them there hills."

This led to a full-scale gold rush. Thousands of men went to Alaska to find gold. The mountainous terrain and bitter climate made the search a huge challenge. Mining was very difficult since the ore was distributed unevenly and digging was slowed by the permafrost. Living in isolated areas with unsanitary conditions led to fires and epidemics.

I visited Pioneer Park in Fairbanks, the site of a large-scale model of a mining operation. The amount of effort and work it took to mine gold was incredible. The miners often had to dig down more than one hundred feet to find gold. The permafrost that far north was almost as hard as rock, and then as they dug, it would become wet.

The next day they would have to deal with the wetness and more rock-hard soil. Once they found gold mixed with dirt and sediment, they had to transport it back to the surface. There they began the process of separating the elements to get the gold.

The level of commitment and sacrifice shown by these men was remarkable. They were willing to do just about anything to find the elusive precious metal. First Peter 1:7 (NLT) says that *your faith is far more precious than mere gold.* Do we act as if our faith is much more valuable than gold? Are we willing to make exceptional sacrifices for Jesus? Will we work as hard as possible to see God's kingdom expand?

If our faith is of such value to us, it should reflect in what we do. Our priorities should match our professed faith. What we are committed to lasts forever, and nothing should be more important to us than eternal souls.

Let's have a "faith rush" for Jesus.

NEVER FORGET

The Lord is . . . not wanting anyone to perish,
but everyone to come to repentance.
—2 PETER 3:9 (NIV)

I was deeply moved by my visit to the 9/11 Museum in New York City. It was one of the more sobering experiences of my life—and I have done many funerals, including those of children. There is just something about the number of lives lost, the inhumanity of the terrorism, and the location in our country's largest city that amplifies the offensiveness of what occurred on September 11, 2001.

Of course, there were bright spots amid the darkness. The sacrificial nature of firefighters, police officers, and civilians was very uplifting. The way the people of New York came together to help each other was inspiring. The show of unity from Americans all across the nation revealed the best of human nature.

The predominant thought that went through my mind as I toured the museum was that you never know when a person's life might end—eternity matters. The verse that came to my mind was 2 Peter 3:9 (NIV): *The Lord is . . . not wanting anyone to perish, but everyone to come to repentance.*

Suffering is a part of this life, but it does not need to be a part of eternity. God wants everyone to spend eternity in heaven with Him. People need to know where they are going when this life ends. They need to know how to get to heaven.

It is our responsibility as Christ followers to share the gospel. People must hear the good news in an understandable way. They need to know that God loves them, has a plan for their life, and will forgive them if they ask Him to. They need to know that they can live an abundant life on this earth and have eternal life in heaven when this life is over.

They need to accept Jesus Christ as their personal Savior and receive forgiveness for their sins. There are many good works we can do in Jesus' name, but other organizations and companies can do them as well. Providing clean water, clothing, and food is very important. Helping stop human trafficking, bringing justice for the incarcerated, and caring for the homeless are certainly important and worthwhile, but only we can proclaim the gospel.

There needs to be a greater burden for souls and a greater urgency to share the gospel. We do not know what tomorrow holds for our family, friends, neighbors, and coworkers. We hope they will be spared tragedy and suffering, but we do not know the future.

What we do know is that they need Jesus in their lives, and we can be the ones to share the good news with them. Never forget it!

NEW LIFE

I tell you for certain that you must be born from above
before you can see God's kingdom!
—JOHN 3:3

We recently experienced something for the very first time: our first grandchild was born. It is always exciting to experience something for the first time, but some "firsts" are more exciting than others—and this one was pretty momentous.

However, it was not without challenge and difficulty. Our son, Matt, and daughter-in-law, Vicky, went to the hospital at 4:30 on a Saturday morning. Michelle and I arrived a few hours later. Not too much was happening, and the wait began—waiting and more waiting. I left the hospital several times, came back, and still waited.

The doctor eventually said that if Vicky did not deliver soon, the baby would have to be delivered by Caesarean section. But a half hour later, at 11:30 p.m., Leo was born. He arrived with the umbilical cord wrapped around his neck. He was literally blue.

He was taken to the Neonatal Intensive Care Unit. Fortunately, he was able to go home after two days.

I couldn't help but reflect on this experience as it relates to spiritual birth. Jesus said in John 3:3, *I tell you for certain that you must be born from above before you can see God's kingdom!*

I was struck by the connection between natural birth and spiritual birth. Giving birth is not easy. The wait for baby Leo to arrive was long and exhausting. Not all births are this way. Some happen more quickly and easily, but this one was a marathon rather than a sprint.

Waiting for someone you know or love to be born again can be arduous. Maybe your spouse has still not accepted Christ, or your friend has come to church but still hasn't been saved. It is hard to wait.

Maybe someone you know has gone through some tough experiences, such as addiction, divorce, or illness. Maybe they have messed up their life with bad choices and unwise actions. The enemy has them around the neck until finally they are born again. You wish it could have been easier, but it wasn't.

What a joy, though, when a loved one is finally born (physically) or born again (spiritually)! The happiness we felt when our grandson was born is hard to put into words, and the happiness you feel when someone you know or love is born again is equally thrilling.

Knowing that you have a new member in your family is like nothing else—except for knowing that there is a new member in God's family. Seeing new life is the best, and it is certainly God's plan. He wants His family to grow. Be a part of it and experience the joy.

THIS IS LIVING

NO REGRETS

"Here comes that dreamer!" they said to each other. "Come
now, let's kill him . . . Then we'll see what comes of his dreams."
—GENESIS 37:19–20 (NIV)

N o regrets." I heard that many times during my athletic career.
It always motivated me and made me want to give the
maximum effort. I have carried the mantra with me throughout
my adult life.

The problem, of course, is that everyone has regrets. You
cannot do everything right, and we all make mistakes. With more
life experience comes greater insight about choices we have made
or actions we have taken.

It turns out that what we regret most is not what we have done
but what we did not do. Cornell University psychologists surveyed
hundreds of participants in six studies, asking them to name their
biggest regret in life. Seventy-six percent said that their biggest
regret was not fulfilling their ideal self.

The researchers identified three elements that make up a person's sense of self. Your "actual self" consists of the qualities you
believe you possess. Your "ought self" is the person you feel you

should be with your responsibilities and obligations. Your "ideal self" is made up of the qualities you want to have. In other words, when it comes to our dreams and aspirations, we fail to act on them, and then later in life we are filled with regret about it. We are quicker to take steps to rectify failures regarding our responsibilities and obligations than to fulfill our dreams and goals.

In the short term, we regret our actions more than our inactions, but in the long term, it is the inaction that leads to greater regret. It is vital to act on our hopes and dreams. Putting them off indefinitely will positively lead to regret later.

Having a vision for your life is the beginning point. An excellent definition of *vision* is "seeing the invisible." Unlike physical vision, this vision is something you can see for your life yet it is not yet visible in your life. When you act on your vision, you will experience opposition. Joseph experienced this. In Genesis 37:19–20 (NIV) we read, *"Here comes that dreamer!" they said to each other. "Come now, let's kill him. . . . Then we'll see what comes of his dreams."*

People will usually try to hinder your dream through criticism and discouragement, but don't let that stop you. Your dream may tap into the insecurities of others, and they may react with words of criticism or may take actions to discourage you.

Act in spite of the opposition. Let the pursuit of your dream shape you. The pain will make you more compassionate, the struggle will make you more patient, and the support will make you humbler.

Whatever is the vision for your life, act on it now. You won't regret it.

NOW, NOT LATER

If you worry about the weather and don't plant seeds,
you won't harvest a crop.
—ECCLESIASTES 11:4

Something happened to our microwave earlier this year. It did not stop working, but it made a loud noise every time it was used. I had a repairman come. He told me that the magnetron had gone bad and that it would cost $300 to fix. I knew I could buy a new microwave for half that amount, but my wife wanted the built-in microwave to work. I didn't want to spend $300 to fix it, so we just left everything the way it was.

Of course, that meant there was an irritating noise every time we used the microwave. When my wife used the microwave, I would go outside or to another part of the house. The sound was very loud and unpleasant, but months went by and nothing changed.

Then the control board on the oven broke, and we had to get it fixed. The repairman told us how much the oven repair would cost. He also told us that the transformer had gone bad in the microwave and would have to be replaced along with the magnetron, adding another $200 to the bill. In order to have a working oven and microwave, I ended up paying almost $1,000.

Are you putting up with something irritating, unpleasant, or damaging in your life? Maybe it hasn't just been going on for a year but for many years. You have allowed it to continue, even though it should have been fixed a long time ago. What will it take for you to finally take action?

Ecclesiastes 11:4 says, *If you worry about the weather and don't plant seeds, you won't harvest a crop.* I was ultimately forced to do something because along with the microwave, my oven broke as well. I should have had the microwave fixed earlier, but I didn't, so I had to have both appliances fixed whether I was financially prepared to or not.

If you don't deal with what is in your life right now, you may end up having to deal with it later when the timing isn't good. Then you will have no choice about it.

If you don't fix, repair, or eliminate whatever is negatively affecting your life, it may end up costing you a lot more later on. No matter how hard or difficult it may be to take action now, imagine how much more it might end up costing you in the future.

Take action today. Don't let more time go by without dealing with what needs to change in your life.

THE FOG OF WORRY

I will make you strong, as I protect you with my arm
and give you victories.

—ISAIAH 41:10

The term "fog of war" is used in military circles to describe the pressures and uncertainties of combat. In a similar way, we are in a war right now against an invisible enemy. The COVID-19 virus is wreaking havoc and spreading incredible fear. People are filled with worry about their health, their family, their finances, and much more.

As we go through this pandemic, we might feel as if we are walking through a fog. We do not understand what is happening all around us. Circumstances occur that we have never experienced before. We can feel alone, and sometimes we are alone. We may even feel as if no one cares. We can't see how we are going to make it through the crisis we are facing.

When fog surrounds us, we are not sure of what lies ahead. Fog is dangerous because it causes us to question what we know to be true. The fog of these present circumstances can tempt us to doubt God and His work in our lives. We long to see as far ahead as possible (certainly to know when this crisis will end), yet all we see is fog.

In such times of intense fog, we can be assured of God's presence and goodness. We can trust God's leading for the next step. Corrie ten Boom once said, "Faith is like radar that sees through the fog—the reality of things at a distance that the human eye cannot see." God wants us to have faith to take the next step of obedience.

Imagine a fog that blankets a city for seven square blocks and to a height of one hundred feet. Fog that deep can cause you to stop moving forward since you cannot see in front of you. However, if you were to take that fog and change it into water, it would fill only a single glass!

We can be so filled with worry right now that it seems as if the fog is seven blocks wide and one hundred feet deep. With God on our side, though, we can see this present crisis as a glass of water, and we will overcome it. As Isaiah 41:10 tells us, *I will make you strong, as I protect you with my arm and give you victories.*

Our faith is certainly being tested, but we serve a God whose name is power. He is able to help us win this war. We need to fight our worries, see through the fog in faith, and trust God to bring us the victory.

NOTHING CAN STOP US

I will build my church, and the gates of Hades will not overcome it.
—**MATTHEW 16:18** (NIV)

A number of years ago, I traveled to Tallinn, Estonia, for a speaking tour. Tallinn is the capital city and cultural hub of the country. Tallinn's Old Town is one of the finest medieval cities in Europe. The only city I have visited that is similar is Bruges, Belgium. Experiencing these incredibly well-preserved medieval cities is like taking a trip back in time.

I went to Tallinn to teach at a Bible college and to preach in several places. One of the places I preached in was a church that met in the former Communist Party headquarters. The building was huge and had a very large auditorium where the church service was held.

Even though it has been years since I ministered there, I have never forgotten it. The auditorium was where the Communists met, and now it was where a church met.

The irony could not be missed, and the differences could not be more stark. Communism is based on the belief that there is no God, there is no supernatural, and there is no fixed morality.

Christianity is based on the exact opposite beliefs: God, the supernatural, and morality are linchpins of a Christian worldview.

Jesus said in Matthew 16:18 (NIV), *I will build my church, and the gates of Hades will not overcome it.* The church continues to grow and expand, while Communism has shrunk and for all intents and purposes is dead. Cuba and Venezuela are essentially Socialist countries. China is supposedly Communist, but China is experiencing economic prosperity only by refuting Marx and his godless philosophy.

Communism failed in Russia and throughout the world. China is atheist, secularist, and humanist—but not Communist. Communism is dead, while the church lives on. The very place that once held Communist meetings now holds church services. The church is victorious over every false belief and worldview.

It may not seem like we are always winning. There is much in culture that is concerning, and the church is certainly challenged by postmodernist beliefs promoted in education, media, and entertainment. An entire generation has been influenced by falsehoods, but we have been here before.

There was a time when it appeared that Communism was winning. Communists were once taking control of major countries in the world, but those days are now long gone. The influence of the church is still seen around the world. Growth is not the same in all places, but there is impact everywhere. The gospel continues to be proclaimed, and nothing can stop the church of Jesus Christ.

THIS IS **LIVING**

THE KEY TO VICTORY

No one in this world always does right.
— ECCLESIASTES 7:20

Phil Mickelson became a major golf champion at age 50 by winning the 2021 PGA Championship. This was his sixth major tournament victory. It was a win for the ages, and he is the oldest major champion in history.

His win was beyond unlikely. Mickelson had not even finished in the top 20 of any tournament this season. He was ranked 115 in the world and was winless the past two years.

He is old enough to play on the senior tour and to many experts, far too old to win on the PGA Tour again—let alone win a major. He had not won a major in eight years; he had not even contended in a major in five years.

But Mickelson believed he could do it. He said after his victory, "This is just an incredible feeling because I believed it was possible, but everything was saying it wasn't."

What was the key to his success? Was it his belief that he could do it? In the interview after his victory, Mickelson said the key was his love of the game and willingness to put in the work.

But the key is really found in something he tweeted just two weeks before the tournament: "I've failed many times in my life and career and because of this I've learned a lot. Instead of feeling defeated countless times, I've used it as fuel to drive me to work harder. So today, join me in accepting our failures. Let's use them to motivate us to work even harder."

Ecclesiastes 7:20 tells us, "No one in this world always does right." The key is how we respond to failure, and failure is a part of life. We cannot always win; losing is a reality. The key is in how we handle failing.

Failure isn't final. It only becomes final when we become negative and quit trying, when we are not brave and courageous. When we keep trying, risking, and advancing, we can have a victory.

Failure is simply feedback—it shows us what doesn't work. It is a marvelous educator. The great thing about failure is that it teaches us, "Don't do that again." Failure coaches us to do it a different way. It shows us what doesn't work and forces us to find new approaches.

The blessing of failure is that it causes us to evaluate our lives. It opens us up to new directions. There is nothing like a setback to cause you to reflect, to cause you to be introspective. Failure has benefits and those benefits can help you to make a comeback.

ONE NAME WILL LIVE FOREVER

At the name of Jesus everyone will bow down,
those in heaven, on earth, and under the earth.
—PHILIPPIANS 2:10

In 1922, British archaeologist Howard Carter discovered King Tutankhamun's tomb in the Valley of the Kings in Egypt. The discovery made headlines around the world. What most impressed people was not King Tut's mummy but the treasures buried with him. The remarkable number of valuables and their incredible preserved state captivated the world. I have been privileged to see some of them.

Tutankhamun was the son of King Akhenaten. Egypt grew weak politically during Akhenaten's thirteen-year reign, and Tutankhamun became king when he was very young. He had a ten-year reign and died when he was just nineteen years old.

Despite countless theories, King Tut's death remains a mystery. Was he a victim of malaria? Could it have been gangrene from a broken leg? Had he been run over by a chariot or gored by a hippo? Whatever the cause of his death, the king was hastily buried and quickly forgotten.

The rulers who followed erased his name from Egypt's important list of kings. They specifically tried to take away all memory of him by not including his name in later lists of kings. They made it as if he never existed.

The living were supposed to continue to speak King Tut's name. Statues and temples were to be built in honor of him. Priests were to mention his name each day. Yet this did not happen. Any record of his name was erased from the royal list.

In fact, King Tut's successors removed every trace of his name. Any monument to him was demolished. Anything that had his name on it was destroyed. Even the funerary cult that existed to remember the dead pharaoh was disbanded.

Written out of history, his name was forgotten. It remained that way for more than thirty-three hundred years—until Howard Carter discovered his tomb. Now Tutankhamun is the most famous king of Egypt. His name is known throughout the world.

I can't help but think about the King of kings as the world increasingly looks to diminish the name of Jesus. The secular push to remove God's name from public mention is strong and growing. The goal is to erase the name of Jesus from the public square.

However, Philippians 2:10 tells us, *At the name of Jesus everyone will bow down, those in heaven, on earth, and under the earth.* The day will come when the greatest name in the world will be Jesus. Everyone will bow before Him. The whole world will acknowledge that Jesus is the King of kings.

PROFILE OF COURAGE

I don't care what happens to me, as long as I finish the work the Lord Jesus gave me to do.
—ACTS 20:24

Paul has been called "the apostle to the nations." He was the greatest follower of Christ in history. He took the gospel to much of the known world in the first century. Largely because of Paul's ministry, Christianity spread throughout the earth and now numbers more than two billion people.

The courage it took to spread the gospel was immense. Paul faced innumerable challenges, but nothing stopped him. He said in Acts 20:24, *I don't care what happens to me, as long as I finish the work the Lord Jesus gave me to do. And that work is to tell the good news about God's great kindness.*

Paul faced opposition everywhere he went, but nowhere more so than in Ephesus. He stayed there for three years—longer than anywhere else. Just the sheer amount of time meant more challenges. He strategically chose Ephesus. Situated in modern-day Turkey, it was the capital city of Asia Minor. It was also the third greatest city of the Roman empire at the time, along with Rome and Alexandria.

During his three years of ministry in Ephesus, Paul preached the gospel, baptized many Christians, performed great miracles, and developed many leaders. He had great success building this key church.

Ephesus was the home of the temple of Diana (known as Artemis in Greek). The structure was one of the Seven Wonders of the Ancient World. People came from all over to worship at Ephesus. I visited the twenty-four-thousand-seat arena where the people gathered to accuse Paul and sought to harm him.

The introduction of Christianity upset the temple priests and the silversmiths who made idols and earned revenue from the cult of Artemis. They accused Paul of being a troublemaker and roused the people against him. Fortunately, the secretary of the city intervened, and Paul was released. Paul experienced this same kind of trouble in Philippi, Corinth, and other places where he preached the gospel.

It would be good for us to follow Paul's example of courage and boldness. He did not let anything stand in his way. Even economic issues could not deter him. I wonder if we would continue to do God's work if financial issues arose. I would like to think we would, but it takes a lot of courage to put God first—especially when money is involved.

Often when we face opposition, we quit. Paul was committed to finishing what he started. It is likely that in the future we will face increased opposition to the gospel. We need to decide today that we will exercise the courage needed to do God's work.

THIS IS **LIVING**

PUTTING THE PUZZLE TOGETHER

Trust in the LORD with all your heart and lean not on your own understanding; in all your ways submit to him, and he will make your paths straight.
—PROVERBS 3:5–6 (NIV)

Soon after our first grandchild was born, a family in our church gave us a puzzle as a Christmas present. They knew that our newly expanded family would be together for the first time at Christmas. They probably thought it would be fun for all of us to do a puzzle together.

Well, we had never done a puzzle before as a family—not once. And this wasn't just any puzzle—it was a Van Gogh painting. It was one where the blue color of the sky dominated a good portion of the painting. In other words, it was hard, especially for novices like us.

My oldest child, Matt, and my daughter-in-law, Vicky, gave it a try, as did my youngest, Wes, and my wife, Michelle. I never even messed with it. They had quite a time just getting the border pieced together. In fact, they had almost given up when my wife took one more shot at it and finally figured it out.

Then it was time to start filling in the pieces. They quickly lost Matt, but they still spent some time on it. Soon Wes bailed, and then my wife quit also. Only Vicky was left to tackle it all by herself. She was also caring for our new grandson, so that puzzle never got completed.

After everyone flew home, the puzzle remained on the dining room table. Soon it was time to take all the Christmas decorations down and put them away. That meant that the puzzle pieces were picked up and put back in the box.

In a similar way as those unfinished jigsaw pieces, we will never see the whole puzzle of our life put together. God wants us to simply take one piece at a time and try to fit it together, and He wants us to believe that He knows what is best for us. Proverbs 3:5–6 (NIV) tells us, *Trust in the LORD with all your heart and lean not on your own understanding; in all your ways submit to him, and he will make your paths straight.*

As our family struggled to finish the border of our puzzle, we wondered if maybe a piece was missing. But then Michelle looked at it from another perspective and saw how it fit together. In a situation like that, you have to believe that the company has put all the pieces in the box that are needed to complete the puzzle. That is their job.

It is the same way with God. We need to trust Him that every piece in our lives is there for a reason. That is God's job, and He knows what He is doing.

QUARANTINED BY DISCRIMINATION

"Lord, you have the power to make me well, if only you wanted to." Jesus put his hand on the man and said, "I want to! Now you are well."
—MATTHEW 8:2–3

Kalaupapa National Historical Park sits on a secluded peninsula separated from the rest of the island of Molokai, Hawaii, by a two-thousand-foot-tall wall of cliffs. There are no roads connecting the peninsula to the top side of Molokai; access is only by aircraft, boat, or mule.

For a century, Kalaupapa was the quarantine site for people afflicted with Hansen's disease, or leprosy. Today it is home to fewer than a dozen former Hansen's disease patients. They are the only residents remaining from the thousands who once lived there, exiled under the quarantine law called the "Act to Prevent the Spread of Leprosy."

Being quarantined by infectious COVID-19 is no fun, but the quarantine lasts just ten to fourteen days. Hansen's disease is a chronic infectious disease caused by bacteria. It is spread in a similar way as COVID-19—by prolonged close contact with an infected person through vapor droplets from the nose and mouth.

Leprosy can now be treated with a multi-drug therapy, but when it first arrived in Hawaii there was no cure. From 1865 to 1969, some eight thousand Hawaiians suspected of having Hansen's disease were forcibly sent to the Kalaupapa peninsula to fend for themselves.

The quarantine law was lifted in 1969, but some of the remaining patients who were cured and allowed to leave did not leave. They knew they would face hardship and discrimination if they left. Those who did leave were turned away from businesses and restaurants. People still treated them differently, being afraid to touch them or to be near them.

The stigma associated with leprosy goes all the way back to biblical times. Lepers were common in the ancient world. They were quarantined and treated as outcasts with no hope of getting well, but Jesus reached out to them on multiple occasions.

Matthew 8:2–3 says, *Suddenly a man with leprosy came and knelt in front of Jesus. He said, "Lord, you have the power to make me well, if only you wanted to." Jesus put his hand on the man and said, "I want to! Now you are well."*

Our response to any group or person who faces discrimination should be similar to the response of Jesus. He reached out with love and healing. A Christlike response to prejudice is compassion. How can we show solidarity with those who are mistreated because of their skin color?

We should acknowledge their pain and seek ways to change behaviors and systems that promote racism. We should help to bring truth, justice, and equality to our community.

SOAR WITH GOD'S POWER

His power at work in us can do far more
than we dare ask or imagine.
—EPHESIANS 3:21

The Andean condor weighs up to thirty-three pounds and has a wingspan stretching ten feet. It is the heaviest soaring bird in the world. Scientists strapped recording equipment on eight birds in Patagonia and recorded more than 250 hours of flight time.

What they discovered was incredible. The condors spent just 1 percent of their time aloft flapping their wings, mostly during take-off. One bird flew farther than one hundred miles in a little more than five hours without ever flapping its wings.

The sky is not empty to these birds but is filled with invisible features such as wind gusts, currents of rising warm air, and streams of air pushed upward by mountains. These amazing birds basically just soar and almost never flap their wings.

Riding the air currents allows the Andean condors to travel long distances while minimizing the exertion of beating their wings. Their exceptional skill at soaring is essential for their scavenger lifestyle.

They circle hours a day over high mountains in their search for a meal of carrion. As they circle, they take advantage of the thermal uplifts—the rising gusts of warm air. This allows them to stay aloft long enough to find food to eat.

These birds exert little effort and yet gain outstanding results. They have mastered the art of soaring, and they reap the benefits of provision for their needs. There is much we can learn from them.

Ephesians 3:21 tells us, *His power at work in us can do far more than we dare ask or imagine.* Too often we try to provide for our needs ourselves instead of relying on God's power. We struggle, we worry, and we labor—all within our own power. We try to solve our problems without God's help.

We know little of living in 1 percent personal effort and 99 percent God's power. If anything, it is the exact opposite. We often can have a meager amount of God's power in our lives, yet His invisible power at work in us can do so much more than we even think is possible.

God calls us to soar, not to strive. He wants us to rest in His unlimited power instead of in our limited strength. We have the Spirit's power available to us, and when we ask for God's help, we will receive it.

So much of what we struggle with could be taken care of by God. All we have to do is stop striving and scheming—and trust that God is able to do it.

TAKEN FOR GRANTED

So I never stop being grateful for you,
as I mention you in my prayers.
—**EPHESIANS 1:16**

The last couple of months have been different for me and my wife. Twice I have traveled for ministry trips, and twice she has traveled to visit family. Over the last seventy days, we have spent twenty days apart—so we have not been together about 30 percent of the time.

I have been traveling for years, but this is different. My trips have generally been shorter, or if they were longer, they were spaced out more. My wife rarely travels without me, and certainly not twice in a short period of time.

I've learned that it is one thing when you are the one away from home and another when you are the one alone at home. I have always missed my wife when I am traveling. In fact, I stopped doing long overseas ministry trips because I did not like being away from home for so long.

However, being the one at home has given me a new perspective. I have come to appreciate just how much my wife does for me. I have a very busy schedule of leading, speaking, and writing. I may not be home that much, and then when I am home, I have writing to do.

My wife takes care of shopping, cooking, laundry, and much more. I do my part by taking care of the finances, handling the home repairs, and planning vacations. In the daily household routine, my wife carries the larger load. The two recent times I have been home alone showed me how much I take her for granted. It is more than the things done, though; I miss the conversations and companionship the most.

Ephesians 1:16 says, *So I never stop being grateful for you, as I mention you in my prayers.* When someone is always around, you can easily take them for granted. If they are there for you and care for you day in and day out, it is so easy to think it will always be this way—until it is not. Then you realize just how much you have taken them for granted.

Is there someone you are taking for granted? It could be your spouse or a friend. Have you thought about all they do to make your life easier or better? Maybe you take your parents for granted. Do you just assume they will always be there for you and will always help when you need it? Could it be your pastor? Do you appreciate his hard work that blesses you in so many ways, along with all the sacrifices he makes?

Make sure people know how much you value them, and don't ever take them for granted.

TAKING A BREAK FROM GOD

Stay joined to me, and I will stay joined to you . . .
I am the vine, and you are the branches.
—JOHN 15:4–5

I'm taking a break from God." Those words have reverberated in my mind for weeks. Those were the words that had been uttered in response to my inquiry about one of our young adults whom I had not seen in church or serving others for a while.

During my years of pastoring, I have sometimes heard, "I'm taking a break from serving." I have even heard, "I'm taking a break from church." But I had never before heard anyone say they were taking a break from God. Maybe she meant that she was taking a break from serving or a break from church—but that is not what she said.

Summer is predicated on taking a break. Many people have a summer vacation as a way to take a break—to relax, rejuvenate, and recreate. It is healthy to unwind and rest. It does your mind, body, and soul good. I strongly believe in taking breaks from your normal routine. For me it is key to creative thoughts and ideas.

But taking a break from God is something totally different. It is very unhealthy to take a break from God. Jesus said in John 15:4–5, *Stay joined to me, and I will stay joined to you. . . . I am the vine, and you are the branches.*

There are a number of potentially bad outcomes when we take even a brief separation from God. We could end up falling into some kind of sin. When we are not in a right relationship with God, the power of temptation could overpower us. Before we know it, we could end up in real trouble, for we are always just one dumb move away from a train wreck.

When not surrounded by our Christian friends, we are susceptible to falling in with the wrong people. They might influence you in a negative way, and just one stupid decision could ruin your life.

Breaking your relationship with God increases your chances of missing out on His favor in your life. God could give you a marvelous opportunity, but if you are not connected to Him—as the vine is connected to the branches—you could miss it.

While we are on a break from God, we are also on a break from His blessings. As a result, we will not be in the right position with the right attitude to take the right action.

Whatever you do, don't ever take a break from God. You may need a break in other areas of your life, but you will never need a break from God. Always stay close to Jesus because He will never take a break from you.

THIS IS **LIVING**

141

RESIST THE FEAR

I asked the LORD for help, and he saved me from all my fears.
—**PSALM 34:4**

Everywhere we turn these days, we see disturbing events unfolding—from mutating viruses to ISIS-K to hurricanes and fires ravaging the land. But Psalm 34:4 says, *I asked the LORD for help, and he saved me from all my fears.*

I believe that the biggest issue people struggle with is fear during normal circumstances, which is especially rampant now. Do we see a difference between those who claim to be followers of Christ and how we are dealing with all the things that are happening in our world? Is there a clear distinction between Christ followers and those who don't have faith?

Resist being fear-filled. Resist it. Fear breeds fear. The more we focus on it, the more exaggerated and distorted the fear becomes. The worst thing you can do is to be fear-focused.

Becoming filled with fear causes fear to breed upon itself and expand and reproduce. Giving in to fear only breeds more fear in our lives. Fear creates spiritual amnesia as we forget all the good things God has done. We seem to forget all the ways God has carried us through. We can get so focused on the world's present crises that we forget. We become spiritual amnesiacs as we forget how God has brought us through time and time again.

As fear begins to take hold, security becomes our god. When our true god is security and safety, we seek out the safest thing, the safest place, and the most secure feeling.

We miss out on so much that God has for us if we try to build safety walls—if we try to hunker down into our bunkers to make everything safe. We cannot create security and safety for ourselves, however, no matter how hard we try.

While we focus on security and safety, opportunities pass us by. Good things don't even get noticed. That is what is so dangerous about this stressful time that we are in right now.

Fear corrodes our confidence in the goodness of God. Either God is good or He isn't. If He is good, then we don't need to be afraid. We have to resist fear—to choose faith over fear. It is a choice. We must choose not to give in to fear.

If we give in to fear, we will miss out on the good things God has for us! We won't even be able to see them because our sole focus will be on safety and security.

Don't do it. Resist giving in to fear.

IT NEVER HAPPENS—EVER

I will never desert you, nor will I ever forsake you.
—HEBREWS 13:5 (NASB)

The Atacama Desert is a plateau in South America that covers a six-hundred-mile strip of land on the Pacific coast west of the Andes Mountains. According to estimates, the Atacama Desert proper occupies forty-one thousand square miles, or forty-nine thousand square miles if the barren lower slopes of the Andes Mountains are included.

The desert is composed of stony terrain, salt lakes, sand, and felsic lava that flows toward the Andes. Much of the desert extends up into the Andes and is very high in elevation. Unlike more familiar deserts like the Sahara Desert in Africa and the Mojave in California, the Atacama is actually a pretty cold place. The average daily temperature ranges between 32° and 72° Fahrenheit.

Studies conducted by NASA have concluded that this desert is in fact the driest place in the world. Evidence suggests that the Atacama Desert may not have had any significant rainfall from 1570 to 1971! Some weather stations in the Atacama have never, ever received rain.

The Atacama is on the northern coast of Chile, right next to the Pacific Ocean—the biggest body of water on Earth. Geographically, the arid nature of the Atacama is explained by it being situated between two mountain chains (the Andes and the Chilean Coast Range) that are of sufficient height to prevent moisture from either the Pacific or the Atlantic Oceans. It is a two-sided rain shadow.

The Atacama is a desert not just because the mountains make a rain shadow, but because the ocean does too. The water on the west part of Chile is quite cold since it comes up from Antarctica. Moisture cannot stay in the cold air above the cold water, so mainly fog reaches the land, but very little rain, if any.

I never knew there was a place in the world where it did not rain. In fact, I did not think it was possible. I assumed that everywhere on Earth received rain in varying degrees. This made me think about what else there is in this world that never happens but we think it does.

Hebrews 13:5 (NASB) tells us, *I will never desert you, nor will I ever forsake you.* Jesus will always be faithful, loyal, caring, merciful, and powerful. You can always trust Jesus. He will never give up on you.

God is loving. God is able. God is in control. Nothing takes God by surprise. God can use anything for our good, and He never makes mistakes. You can count on it. You can count on Him.

THE CHURCH IS
THE LIGHTHOUSE

I am the light for the world! Follow me, and you won't be
walking in the dark. You will have the light that gives life.
—JOHN 8:12

Many times when God speaks, He uses physical images or
pictures to show us spiritual truth. One picture God gave
me was when I was at the beach and was visiting a lighthouse.

Many people, including me, like to visit lighthouses. They are
always on the water and are often in beautiful places. For years we
vacationed as a family on Cape Cod, and the town we stayed in
had a beautiful lighthouse we would often visit. Lighthouses are
nice to look at, but that, of course, is not their purpose.

A lighthouse is not needed when the sun is shining and the
seas are calm. A lighthouse is needed when it is dark and there
are storms. In our culture today, it is dark and there are storms.
It is dark and there are storms today in many people's lives. Our
neighbors need a lighthouse, our friends need a lighthouse, and
our coworkers need a lighthouse. The church is the lighthouse.

Jesus said in John 8:12, *I am the light for the world! Follow me, and you won't be walking in the dark. You will have the light that gives life.* Jesus is the light, and the church is the lighthouse. We shine the light of Jesus into our community and the world. When people come to Jesus, He gives them life—abundant life on this earth and eternal life in heaven.

Lighthouses have amazing light power. The light from the Cape Hatteras Lighthouse on the Outer Banks of North Carolina can be seen twenty miles away. It is remarkable that a ship twenty miles from shore can see the light that will guide them to safety.

The light of Jesus is even more powerful. His light can guide people out of their confusion, out of their denial, and out of their hopelessness. Jesus saves lost people, and He uses His lighthouse, the church, to do it.

People need the Lord. We know them, we work with them, we live near them, and we are related to them. We must invite them to church and to Jesus. We cannot wait for them to come on their own. Today is the day of salvation. The time to bring your friends to church is now.

Churches are not built to transfer in Christians from other churches, in which case the kingdom of God is not expanded but only rearranged. We must reach the lost and shine the light of Jesus. Commit to this God-ordained, Great Commission-fulfilling, gospel-proclaiming vision.

THE CURE

The heart is deceitful above all things, and desperately wicked.
—JEREMIAH 17:9 (NKJV)

There is much to see in Munich, Germany, but there is an unprecedented place to visit just outside the city. That place is Dachau, the first concentration camp built by the Nazis. When my wife and youngest son traveled with me to Germany, my son asked if we could skip the visit to Dachau because it would be so depressing.

He was right about it being depressing, but I thought it had to be done. Depressing only scratches the surface of how awful it was. Nothing can really prepare you for what you will witness. The level of human sinfulness and depravity is unparalleled.

Dachau was built as a prototype for concentration camps. It was copied in many more camps throughout Germany and Poland. To use words like "prototype" and "copy" to speak of something so vile is incredible. The vastness of such evil is on a scale hard to comprehend.

We watched a film in one of the buildings. What was portrayed was hard to watch and even harder to believe. People were treated so inhumanely. The level of cruelty was beyond imagination. The refusal of basic human rights reflected the Nazis' insane belief that the prisoners were in fact less than human.

The starvation and disease stood out among all the horrors. How could these Nazis watch their fellow countrymen suffer at the most basic level of survival? It is simply a reflection of the evil and wickedness that can inhabit the heart of men. There is no other reasonable explanation.

Six million Jews died in concentration camps. That number is remarkable. How any human being could have done such a thing to their fellow man can only be explained by Jeremiah 17:9 (NKJV): *The heart is deceitful above all things, and desperately wicked.*

The reality is that although no single event as horrendous has happened since the Holocaust, there are plenty of other examples of wickedness—even today. Terrorism is rampant around the world. Evildoers exist on every continent, not to mention the way racism continues to this day.

Sinfulness exists in individual lives as well. I recently witnessed firsthand two examples of sinful behavior that, if I had not seen them for myself, I would have never believed that they could have taken place. It is shocking how we can deceive ourselves into believing that sin is acceptable.

The only cure is Jesus. Only He can change a sinful heart. We have a terminal condition that can only be healed by Jesus. The sole remedy is repentance and forgiveness through Jesus Christ.

Reach out to Him today and have your heart healed.

THE EYE TEST

People judge others by what they look like,
but I judge people by what is in their hearts.
—1 SAMUEL 16:7

Fall is my favorite season of the year for several reasons. One big reason is because of football, which has been a part of my life for many years. There is so much I love about the game. It is the ultimate demonstration of toughness and intellect. The elements it teaches of teamwork, discipline, and hard work provide the foundation for success in life.

In football we have what is called "the eye test." That means that when a team gets off the bus, you take a look at them and see if they pass the test. Do they look like football players? When they take the field before the game without pads, do they look athletic?

This evaluation has nothing to do with whether they can actually play football or if they really are skilled players. It is all based on whether they look like they can play. Only after seeing the players perform can you know if the eye-test evaluation was accurate.

We can do the same thing when we evaluate people, and we often evaluate incorrectly. In 2 Corinthians 5:16 (NIV), Paul says,

So from now on we regard no one from a worldly point of view. Though we once regarded Christ in this way, we do so no longer.

Human beings tend to judge by what they see and perceive. Paul tells us that he stopped evaluating the wrong way.

First Samuel 16:7 tells us the correct way: *People judge others by what they look like, but I judge people by what is in their hearts.* When God sent Samuel to find a new king to replace Saul, he picked Jesse's oldest son, Eliab, because he was tall and handsome, like Saul. However, God chose Jesse's youngest son, David, to be the new king. David was nothing to look at like Saul was. The Bible calls him ruddy. Today he might derisively be called a ginger. David was not particularly impressive physically. He was just a lowly shepherd, yet God picked him to be king.

Appearances can be deceptive. God knows our hearts. They tell the truth about who we really are. Do you treat people differently based on how they look or what they wear? If so, you are evaluating incorrectly. You never really know who that person is simply by their outward appearance.

It is best to treat everybody like a somebody—because they are. Don't let outward appearances cause you to judge wrongly. Treat people with kindness and respect, and let God judge their hearts.

GET IT OUT

Don't let anyone become bitter
and cause trouble for the rest of you.
—HEBREWS 12:15

I recently became very ill. I didn't get diagnosed with a disease or even spend time in a hospital, but I have never been sicker in my life. I contracted a virus. The medical term is gastroenteritis. The southern term is "sick as a dawg."

It started on a Sunday night. I probably got it by shaking hands with tons of people after church and then not properly washing my hands. I do not know how it happened, but all I know is that it was awful.

I woke up around midnight and had to vomit. I probably hadn't vomited in fifteen years. Then two hours later it happened again. This was followed by non-stop diarrhea. I think you get the picture. To make matters worse, my wife was out of town. Then she was supposed to return home on Monday, but her flight was cancelled.

So there I was, sick and alone. It was bad. I hardly ever get sick, and my schedule is not made for sick days. I asked the doctor what could be done. He told me that nothing could be done other than to let it run its course. The most important thing he said was, "Your body wants this gone. It won't stop until this bug is out of your system."

The vomiting and diarrhea continued until the virus was completely out of my body. That took more than three days. Three miserable days. After it was over, I realized how great it is to have health. It made me thankful for how healthy I am and how rarely I get sick.

It also made me think about something else. Sometimes there is stuff that needs to get out of us—not physical stuff, but emotional stuff. I am referring to the stuff that makes us sick in ways other than physically.

Hebrews 12:15 tells us, *Don't let anyone become bitter and cause trouble for the rest of you.* Bitterness can get in your heart and poison you as you become filled with anger about injustice. The unfairness can cause you to be miserable about your own life and envious of the lives of others. You have got to get rid of it or you won't be able to get well.

Instead of being plagued by injustice, perhaps you are plagued by regret. The mistakes you have made can eat away at your soul as you mourn what could have been, and you cannot let it go. You wish things could be different, but they're not. If you don't let it go, your mental health will suffer.

Get rid of it. You can't be healthy until it is gone.

THIS IS **LIVING**

IS THE FIRE STILL BURNING?

There an angel of the LORD appeared to him from a burning bush. Moses saw that the bush was on fire, but it was not burning up.

—EXODUS 3:2

In 1962, a fire started burning in Centralia, Pennsylvania, and has been burning ever since. It is believed that on May 27, 1962, the fire was intentionally set in a waste disposal area. The city council had decided to burn the waste to clean up the landfill, a common practice during that time.

Pennsylvania has some of the largest coal deposits in the world. Centralia is located in the eastern part of the state and was once a town with a busy mining business. It turns out that the landfill was situated on top of an old coal mine, and the fire ignited the coal beneath.

Authorities tried for years to extinguish the fire. They pumped water into the mine, covered the surface with clay, and dumped wet sand into holes drilled down from the surface—but none of those attempts put out the fire.

In the 1980s, state and federal authorities gave up trying to extinguish the fire. Unlike wood in a forest fire, coal burns slowly and steadily. Coal naturally contains its own fuel (carbon), and the tunnels provide oxygen from the surface. The town is all but abandoned, and when the last few people die, no one will ever live there again.

The fire continues to burn below the surface. It now reaches as deep as three hundred feet and covers six square miles. The fire grows fifty to seventy feet per year. Most amazingly, the fire will continue to burn for another one hundred years.

I'm struck by how nothing can put out the fire and that the fire will keep burning for a century.

Can the same be said about us? Is there a fire for God burning within us that can't be extinguished? Will a fire for God keep burning during our entire lives?

God revealed Himself several times in the Bible through fire. It is a symbol of His presence. Exodus 3:2 says, *There an angel of the LORD appeared to him from a burning bush. Moses saw that the bush was on fire, but it was not burning up.*

The fire of God in us means that we want more of God, we desire what He wants, and we have passion. To be fired up for God is to have enthusiasm and zeal for the things of God.

Is the fire still burning in you? Make sure nothing can put it out. If you stay on fire for God, He will continue to do new and powerful things in your life.

THE HALL OF FAME

All of them pleased God because of their faith!
—HEBREWS 11:39

I attended the NFL Hall of Fame enshrinement ceremony in Canton, Ohio, in 2016. My cousin, Eddie DeBartolo, was being inducted for his ownership of the San Francisco 49ers, having led them to five Super Bowl championships. It was a great honor for Eddie to be included in the Hall of Fame. At the ceremony, he talked about how important creating a family environment was to the team's incredible success.

The night also included other inductees, including Brett Favre and Tony Dungy. Both men acknowledged Jesus as their Lord and Savior. Dungy quoted Matthew 16:26: *What would it profit a man to gain the whole world and forfeit his soul?* He said it was his mother, Cleomae, who taught him that verse, and he never forgot it. He also spoke about God's plan for his life and how he found success despite several disappointments.

Every new inductee expressed thanks for the many people who helped them reach the pinnacle of professional football. Parents, coaches, teachers, and friends were mentioned as crucial to the success of these men who were receiving football's highest honor. The entire night was very uplifting and special.

The whole time, my thoughts were about how great it is to be in a hall of fame. I love halls of fame. I enjoy learning about greatness and hearing about people who were excellent. I have visited many halls of fame, both big and small, such as tennis, volleyball, golf, basketball, racing, baseball, and many more. My oldest son, Matt, was born in Springfield, Massachusetts, home of the Naismith Memorial Basketball Hall of Fame.

The reality is that there is a hall of fame that is open to any follower of Christ. It is the "Faith Hall of Fame." Hebrews 11 tells us about the heroes of the faith who are now with God. We read about the lives of these great Old Testament believers whose faith made them pleasing to God. They trusted in the promises of God. Their faith is what got them into the Faith Hall of Fame, and their example is worth following.

Read all of Hebrews 11 to learn about the great faith of these men and women. Hebrews 11:39 sums it up: *All of them pleased God because of their faith!* Our goal should be to have the same kind of faith that our spiritual ancestors had.

There can be no greater honor than to be included in God's hall of fame. If we live our lives walking in faith and obedience, someday we, too, can end up in the Faith Hall of Fame.

THE BIBLE'S IMPACT

Everything in the Scriptures is God's Word. All of it is useful for teaching and helping people and for correcting them and showing them how to live.

—2 TIMOTHY 3:16

I have visited the Museum of the Bible three times: once while it was under construction, once when it first opened, and again recently. The museum is a must-visit for anyone who reads the Bible, hears it preached, and studies what it says. It is the culmination of thirteen years of labor and is the result of a great vision. It is a gift from the generous Greene family—the founders of the Hobby Lobby retail chain—for everyone to enjoy.

Each time I am there, I am reminded anew of the enormous impact the Bible has had on humanity. The museum provides a singular place to experience the multitude of ways the Bible has shaped our world and influenced everything from art to science to government—and of course, religion.

The exhibit on Billy Graham focuses on his use of the Bible in preaching. One of his quotes is, "I've read the last page of the Bible. It's all going to turn out all right." This is what the Bible gives us—hope.

Eighty-seven percent of homes in America have a Bible. The Bible is the best-selling book every single year, and it has been translated into 673 different languages. The YouVersion Bible App has been downloaded to more than three hundred million devices.

But knowing the greatness of the Bible is not enough. Just owning a Bible is not enough. It has to be read and applied. Second Timothy 3:16–17 says, *Everything in the Scriptures is God's Word. All of it is useful for teaching and helping people and for correcting them and showing them how to live. The Scriptures train God's servants to do all kinds of good deeds.*

I estimate that I have preached messages from the Bible about two thousand times, and that does not include the books and articles I have written. There is much in the Bible to learn. It is a reservoir of resources on how to live a good and godly life.

We must dig deeply into it, excavating the timeless treasures waiting for each of us to find. We find unchangeable truths in its pages that help us to see the nature of God and of man.

We continue to study it, allowing God to speak to us. We see the faith, the character, and the mistakes of those who came before us to guide us as we walk our spiritual journey. We use it as an invaluable tool to help craft a workable, practical faith in the world in which we live. As Christ followers, we should read, study, meditate on, and obey the Bible.

THE LAST SUPPER

After Jesus had said these things, he was deeply troubled and told his disciples, "I tell you for certain that one of you will betray me."
—JOHN 13:21

The Last Supper by Leonardo da Vinci is the most famous religious painting in the world. I have always wanted to see it, and while I was in Milan, Italy, I was finally able to do so. I wondered what it would look like since it has a long history of not being cared for properly.

The painting, or more specifically, the mural, is more than five hundred years old. It is on a wall in a refectory, or dining hall. Imagine one of the finest paintings in the world by one of the greatest artists in history being painted on a wall where monks had lunch!

The painting was damaged when the room it was in was used as part of a prison and inmates would throw stones at it. It was also damaged by faulty restoration work as the masterpiece was presumed to be a fresco (it is not, since it was painted on dry plaster). Further degradation was caused by open-air exposure during World War II bombing.

In 1978, a major twenty-one-year renovation began to stabilize the painting, repair damage caused by dirt and pollution, and reverse previous failed restoration attempts from the eighteenth and nineteenth centuries.

The refectory was converted to a sealed climate-controlled environment. On May 28, 1999, the painting was returned to display. Visitors can only stay for fifteen minutes, yet more than half a million people visit the painting every year—and it is worth the visit.

The painting represents the scene of the Last Supper of Jesus with His disciples, recorded in John 13:21: *After Jesus had said these things, he was deeply troubled and told his disciples, "I tell you for certain that one of you will betray me."*

Leonardo's painting is different from previous paintings of the Last Supper because the others focused on the moment of identification of Judas as the traitor. Judas was placed in an isolated position with respect to the other disciples when he received a piece of bread from Christ.

Leonardo da Vinci chose the moment before this in which the traitor had yet to be identified and the disciples expressed shock through the expression of their faces, the posture of their bodies, and the movement of their hands.

Leonardo created a sense of continuity between the space of the refectory and the painting through his use of perspective, with Christ's right temple as the vanishing point. All the lines of perspective guide your eye toward Jesus' face as the center of the work.

When we celebrate communion, the focus is on Jesus, not Judas. The Last Supper is not about betrayal but about sacrifice. The painting appropriately centers on Jesus as the Savior of the world.

THE ONLY WAY TO FINISH

I have not yet reached my goal, and I am not perfect. But
Christ has taken hold of me. So I keep on running and
struggling to take hold of the prize.
—PHILIPPIANS 3:12

In Lausanne, Switzerland, in July 2019, an Ethiopian runner did
something that will not soon be forgotten. Hagos Gebrhiwet was
running in the five-thousand-meter race at the Diamond League
meet when he veered out of his lane toward the crowd. He then
stopped and celebrated his victory—one lap too soon.

Gebrhiwet strode right past the bell for the final lap and then
proceeded to raise his hands in celebration of what he thought
was his first-place finish, all while his fellow competitors ran right
past him. The race continued for another lap, and Yomif Kejelcha
crossed the actual finish line and won the race.

Gebrhiwet is a world-class runner. He earned a bronze medal
at the 2016 Summer Olympics and has two medals from the World
Championships. In this race, though, he didn't run through the finish
line but stopped a lap short. After he realized his mistake, he tried to
make up ground, but he ultimately finished tenth in the event.

None of Gebrhiwet's previous victories or accomplishments could save him from the embarrassment of misjudging the finish line in Lausanne. You are required to run through the finish line. How could a veteran runner forget where the finish line actually was?

The same thing can happen to us as followers of Christ. This is why Paul encourages us in Philippians 3:12: *I have not yet reached my goal, and I am not perfect. But Christ has taken hold of me. So I keep on running and struggling to take hold of the prize.*

The prize is heaven, and until we get there, we are to keep running and striving. God has placed each of us on this earth for a reason, and we are to live out our life's purpose. It may be tempting to stop and begin to celebrate what has been done, but then we run the risk of finishing a lap short. The ultimate victory can only be achieved by crossing the finish line.

It is not how we start but how we finish that matters. Some people don't have a great start, but they can have a great finish. It is encouraging to know that God can continue to work in us our whole lives as long as we don't stop too soon.

Finishing well is the goal. You may be weary, you may be discouraged, and you may want to quit. Don't do it. Keep running with Jesus. Keep serving the Lord. There is a marvelous prize waiting for you in heaven.

THE MYSTERY

Just as the heavens are higher than the earth,
my thoughts and my ways are higher than yours.
—ISAIAH 55:9

Have you heard of *Physarum polycephalum*? It is more commonly known as slime or the blob. This single-celled slime mold has no nervous system, but it can learn, pass knowledge to other molds, and repair itself in minutes. It can navigate without eyes, limbs, or wings. Scientists still don't know how to explain how it does what it does.

They don't know if it is an animal, a fungus, or something in between. It is capable of memory and adapted behavior. It is capable of solving problems. Slime molds are protists—single-celled organisms grouped into their own kingdom on the evolutionary family tree because scientists aren't sure where else to put them.

By looking at the yellowish veins of matter, you wouldn't know that it just might be the most cunning brainless organism on the planet. The organism's informal name comes from the film *The Blob*, a 1958 Steve McQueen movie about a creature from space that consumes two Pennsylvania towns in a bout of alien rage.

Many people want all decisions to be dictated by science—as if science has all the answers. But it doesn't. As we have all seen, scientists often give directives and then change their minds, leaving us wondering which of their opinions is accurate.

I am not anti-science. I have spoken about the harmonious relationship between science and faith. Some of the greatest scientists who ever lived were Christians. I actually enjoy studying quantum physics just to stimulate my thinking and exercise my brain. My youngest son works in the science field. However, science does not have all the answers.

Some people put all their faith in science. These are the people whose religion is scientism. They believe in science with a religious fervor. They are atheistic or agnostic and believe science has the answers to everything. It is hard for them to admit or accept the reality that not everything can be explained.

For a Christ follower, the question may be why the pandemic happened. Was it judgment from God, or was God speaking to us through this crisis? Isaiah 55:8–9 tells us, *The LORD says: "My thoughts and my ways are not like yours. Just as the heavens are higher than the earth, my thoughts and my ways are higher than yours."*

We want to know everything, but not everything can be known. Some things are mysteries only to be known in heaven. In the meantime, we must live with the ambiguity and put our trust in God above science and everything else.

THE PATH OF PROCRASTINATION

If you are too lazy to plow, don't expect a harvest.
—PROVERBS 20:4

Proverbs 20:4 tells us, *If you are too lazy to plow, don't expect a harvest.* Life is too short to procrastinate about things that need to get done.

The German writer Goethe wrote, "Hell begins the day that God grants you the vision to see all you could have done, should have done, and would have done, but did not do." You don't want to live without getting the important stuff done.

The path of procrastination starts with hope. It goes like this: "I'll start early this time." Then we move to tension: "I've got to start soon." Next we move to guilt: "I should have started sooner." After that we move to a false sense of assurance: "Oh, there's still time." Then we move into true panic: "I can't wait any longer." Finally, we end up in resignation: "Next time I'll start earlier."

Time is precious and life is short. Time moves by very quickly, and before you know it, things have happened that you cannot change. You have to identify what is important to you because what is important to me might not be important to you.

Many people confuse the urgent with the important. The urgent gets attention while we procrastinate regarding the important. The things that really matter don't get done because the squeaky wheel gets the grease. Whoever whines the most and cries the loudest gets attention. That is no way to live your life.

I live by this mantra: You don't prioritize your schedule; you schedule your priorities. In other words, you don't look at your schedule and say, "Oh, let me see. What is most important? Let me put that first." That will never work. What you should do is say, "These are my priorities, and I will schedule them in." Priorities get scheduled, and then the important stuff gets done.

Don't allow yourself to go from fire to fire, from crisis to crisis, and from drama to drama where you are in a constant state of what is most urgent. We live in a culture of immediacy. Everything is urgent.

However, the truth is that everything is not urgent. It's not. How do you get the important things done? You do so by not allowing yourself to be pushed around by everyone who says, "My thing is the most important thing."

Determine what is most important—and then do it!

THE SUN WILL RISE
TOMORROW

This hope is like a firm and steady anchor for our souls.
—HEBREWS 6:19

The sun set on November 18, 2020, in Utqiagvik, Alaska (formerly known as Barrow). It did not rise again for another sixty-six days. Polar night brought darkness to America's northernmost town. When the sun finally rose again, there was a new year, a new president, and a new vaccine for COVID-19.

Polar night is a natural phenomenon that happens every year. It occurs each winter because the tilt of the earth's axis means none of the sun's disc is visible above the horizon. This only happens in places within the polar circles.

The sun did not rise again in this Alaskan town until January 23, 2021. It was never total darkness during the day. There were a few hours each day with enough light to see, but the people had seen their last sunset until the next year.

Some Alaskans prepare for this by taking vitamin D supplements. They may choose to have a light that mimics daylight, or they might simply have learned to accept this annual challenge. It certainly is unique and unlike anything most Americans ever experience.

My mom used to give me the following advice whenever something bad happened: "The sun will come up in the morning." Despite the things in my life that seemed disappointing or even awful, the sun would come up the next day. Life would go on, and somehow I would find a way to go on too.

The sun will indeed come up. Tomorrow is a new day. No matter how much darkness there may be in your life, there will be light to break through the darkness. There is always hope for tomorrow, just like the song in the musical *Annie* that says, "The sun will come out tomorrow. . . . You're only a day away."

But what if there is a time when the sun does not come up in the morning for you? What if there are sixty-six (or more) days before the sun comes out again in your life? What if things don't go as planned?

If that happens, then look to Jesus. Depend on Jesus. You don't have to go through dark days alone when He has promised to always be with you.

It is not the hope of tomorrow that we hang on to, but we hang on to the hope that we have in Jesus. He is our sure and steadfast hope. Hebrews 6:19 tells us, *This hope is like a firm and steady anchor for our souls*, and we rely on it, sunrise or not.

THE WARNING

If my own people will humbly pray and turn back to me
and stop sinning, then I will answer them from heaven.
—2 CHRONICLES 7:14

On March 18, 1937, in New London, Texas, a spark ignited a cloud of natural gas that had accumulated in the enclosed crawl space of the Consolidated School building. The blast killed 293 people, most of them children.

The explosion happened because the local school board wanted to cut heating costs. Natural gas, the by-product of petroleum extraction, was siphoned from the residue gas line of the nearby Parade Gasoline Company to fuel the school's gas heaters free of charge.

Natural gas is both odorless and colorless, so the leak was difficult to detect and went unnoticed. When the explosion occurred, the roof was blown off the building and then crashed back down on it.

This was one of the worst disasters involving children in American history. It was a total tragedy and brought incredible heartache to this small east Texas town. To this day, it is a subject that most residents are unwilling to discuss.

However, something very positive came out of this disastrous event. The Texas Legislature mandated that an odorant be added to natural gas, and that requirement quickly spread worldwide.

Now the putrid smell of rotten eggs is familiar to everyone, reminding us that there is natural gas nearby. The strong odor makes leaks quickly detectable. Out of such a great tragedy, many other lives have been saved from an undetected gas leak.

We are living in a time of great challenge and heartache. As of September 2021, more than 650,000 lives (and counting) have been lost in the U.S. alone to the pandemic. This experience can be valuable if it warns us of what needs to change.

Second Chronicles 7:13–14 says, *Suppose I hold back the rain or send locusts to eat the crops or make my people suffer with deadly diseases. If my own people will humbly pray and turn back to me and stop sinning, then I will answer them from heaven.*

What can we learn from this challenging experience? What is it that God may be saying to the church? What might He be saying to our culture? What is He saying to you? This season is like a giant explosion that is blowing up our typical way of living.

We are living in a different reality. Our normal schedule is temporarily gone. Many people don't go to work, kids don't go to school, and we are not allowed to go to church on Sundays.

What needs to change? Is there something we need to add to our lives? Is there something missing? We need to act so that something good can come from all this pain and suffering.

JESUS IS THE CENTER

Christ will rule until he puts all his enemies under his power, and the last enemy he destroys will be death.
—1 CORINTHIANS 15:25–26

Few palaces rival the Palace of Versailles for sheer opulence and size. Before I visited the palace, I did not realize that it is actually more than just a palace, but it is a massive group of buildings and gardens. It would cost thirty-one billion dollars to build today. That number is difficult to even comprehend.

The palace is located on the outskirts of Paris and is the former home of French kings. The complex was commissioned by King Louis XIV, who moved France's government to Versailles in 1682 and wanted a palace to match the glory of his reign.

Nowhere is this more evident than in the Hall of Mirrors. The elegant ballroom spans some 240 feet and is adorned with colossal arched mirrors, gilded statues, and dazzling chandeliers. It is amazing to witness such splendor.

Versailles remained the epicenter of French royal power for more than a century—until 1789. Though the French Revolution ended its governmental use, the palace remains a special place because of its beauty and legacy. It was also where the Treaty of Versailles was signed in June 1919, ending World War I.

King Louis XIV called himself the sun god. He literally believed that everything revolved around him. He had symbols of the sun placed throughout the palace to remind people of who he was. His bedroom was in the very center of the palace so that everyone knew he was to be the center of it all.

He was the only one who had a chair at his table. All the guests sat on the floor so they could look up to him. He had a chapel in the palace where he worshiped every morning, but at Mass he had all the congregants say, "The king is coming" when he entered. The focus was always on him—even in church.

First Corinthians 15:25–26 tells us, *Christ will rule until he puts all his enemies under his power, and the last enemy he destroys will be death.* There is only one king, and His name is Jesus. Everything revolves around Him—not anyone else. His rule continues in this world until His second coming.

Jesus should be the center of our lives. Everything should revolve around Jesus and His will for us. It is all about Jesus—not anything else. Nothing should matter to us more than Him, and our lives should be focused on what He wants more than what we want.

In God's kingdom, Jesus is the king of our lives.

THERE MUST BE
SOMETHING MORE

Then I thought about everything I had done, including the hard work, and it was simply chasing the wind.
—ECCLESIASTES 2:11

I was recently in South Florida. The weather was fantastic and there was natural beauty everywhere. It was hard to come back to snow and sleet. But it wasn't all great. The traffic was crazy, and the focus on pleasure-seeking was easy to see.

When we were in South Beach, we could not miss seeing the Rolls Royce automobiles, luxury shops, and nightclubs. They were everywhere. The party lifestyle is trumpeted in our culture as the best way to live, and South Beach is ground zero for the commonly accepted concept of the good life.

But this cultural view fails to consider the long-term dimensions of life, and it certainly ignores eternal life. Pleasure-seeking has its thrills and fun, but it offers little, if anything, that will last into eternity.

King Solomon would have fit right in with today's culture. He was committed to enjoying pleasure, enlarging his kingdom, acquiring more possessions than everyone else, and getting whatever his heart desired.

Ecclesiastes 2:1, 3 tells us, *I said to myself, "Have fun and enjoy yourself!... I wanted to find out what was best for us during the short time we have on this earth."*

Solomon partied, built a beautiful home, amassed a fortune, had lots of sex, and achieved great fame. He got whatever he wanted and did whatever made him happy. He achieved the ultimate in short-term pleasure and instant gratification, yet he eventually grieved over the outcome of his life. He said in verses 11 and 17, *Then I thought about everything I had done, including the hard work, and it was simply chasing the wind. . . . This made me hate life.*

Solomon's pursuits left him longing for something more. That something more is God.

Faith in God moves you out of a self-centered pursuit of life by introducing you to something bigger than yourself. God has created us to serve Him and others, not to just focus on ourselves. We find significance when we don't live for our own pleasure but for God's. Loving God and others brings the greatest satisfaction.

If you spend your life focused on yourself, you will become enslaved to your own appetites and you will never find the fulfillment you seek. Pleasure can be a delightful servant if it is dedicated to God—but it makes a terrible master.

Which master do you serve? What drives you? Are you squandering your future on short-term pleasure, or are you living for eternity?

TIME TO PRAY

He knelt down in prayer three times a day,
giving thanks to God.
—DANIEL 6:10

Each year we move our clocks forward one hour for daylight saving time. Have you ever thought about who invented clocks or why they were invented?

The Roman Empire began as the Romans took over the major cities of the known world. In every city they conquered, they would build a forum like the one in Rome. I have visited that forum, and it is amazing to see what they built. There were buildings for commercial, political, social, legal, and religious purposes. The forum was the hub of the city.

A bell tower was built in each forum. The Roman bell tower would ring six or seven times a day. It would first ring at 6:00 a.m. This was the first hour of the day and was a signal to get to work. It would also ring at the sixth hour, which was noon. This was the lunch break. The bells continued to ring throughout the day.

We see these terms for the hours of the day in the Bible. For instance, when Jesus was crucified, the Bible says it was the third hour—meaning Jesus was crucified at 9:00 a.m.

Since everyone could hear the bells ringing throughout the day, Christians developed the habit of praying every time the bells rang. To this day, the Catholic Church has the Liturgy of the Hours, using the same Roman terms for the times to pray. As monks began building monasteries, they would construct bell towers so they could ring the bells as a call to prayer.

In the 1400s, the monks decided it would be better to create a mechanical device that would automatically ring the bells on schedule each day. They were successful with their invention. They named it after the Latin word for bell, which is *cloc*. Clocks were invented to make time for prayer.

Daniel 6:10 says, *He knelt down in prayer three times a day, giving thanks to God.* The clock was not invented for business, nor was it invented to make life more organized. It was invented so we would know when it was time to pray. May we never look at our watches or clocks in the same way again!

Now that you know the story of the clock, I hope you will be reminded to pray more. Let the Spirit move you to pray for those you care about. Pray for the needs of your church. Pray about the needs in your own life.

There is much to pray about. Start looking at your clock.

EXPERIENCING FREEDOM

Christ has set us free! . . . Now hold on to your freedom and don't ever become slaves of the Law again.
—GALATIANS 5:1

During a trip to Alaska, we arrived in Fairbanks, checked into our hotel, and then headed out to get some dinner. When it came time to pay, I noticed that the bill did not include any tax. The meal cost exactly the amount shown in the menu. It took me back. A few years ago, the county where I live added a 4 percent meals tax on top of our 5.3 percent sales tax. Whenever we go out to eat, we essentially have to add 10 percent to the cost of our meal.

In Alaska, though, there is no sales tax. I thought this might just apply to meals, so the next day I bought a souvenir—and sure enough, no sales tax on that either. Before we left the following day, I was trying to decide whether or not to buy something. It was expensive but would be a great memento of our trip. The tipping point for me to purchase it was—no sales tax!

The wilderness of Alaska is beautiful, the wildlife is unique, and the combination makes for an unforgettable adventure—but not paying sales tax made an impression on me as well.

This experience caused me to think about what it is like to be free of something. Galatians 5:1 says, *Christ has set us free! This means we are really free. Now hold on to your freedom and don't ever become slaves of the Law again.* When we accept Jesus and receive forgiveness for our sins, the power of sin is broken in our lives. We are free to become who God created us to be. Freedom in Christ is a marvelous way to live.

Sadly, not everyone is free. Far too many people are in bondage, addicted to something. They have a life-controlling problem. It may be alcohol, drugs, overspending, food, gossip, sex, or any number of other issues. They do not know what it is like to be free. They live every day knowing there is something that enslaves them and keeps them from being who they could be.

If only they could experience what it is like to be free! I had been paying sales tax for years, and the moment I didn't have to was thrilling. I was happy to save a little bit of money, but what you will find truly exhilarating is to finally be free from an addiction that controls your life.

The good news is that freedom is possible in Christ, and this freedom is not just located in one place, but it is available anytime, anywhere, for the rest of your life.

FOCUS ON TIMING

It takes careful planning for things to go right.
—PROVERBS 15:22

I recently received a text from my wife while I was out of town. I was at an important luncheon, but I thought what my wife wanted must be important, so when I was free I called her. She had the most incredible story to tell me.

She met someone that day who was from New England. During their conversation, she learned that this woman was from the same small Connecticut town where I am from. Then my wife found out that the woman actually went to high school with me, graduating the same year I did, and that we were actually friends! We had lived in the same city for the last twenty-six years and never knew it. Only an unusual sequence of timing allowed this news to be made known.

Timing is so crucial in life. The late Lee Iacocca once said, "Even the right decision is the wrong decision if it's made at the wrong time." Timing is hugely important in a decision. You could get a decision right, but if you make it at the wrong time, it is a wrong decision.

In making sound decisions, you have to collect all the information, and you have to take your time. When people come to me and want an answer to an important decision right away, I always answer with a no. I'm not going to make a decision when I haven't thought and prayed about it. I can't make a good decision until I first determine if the timing is right.

Take your time. God's will is not just about what to do, but it is also about when to do it. We often focus on the what but not on the when. It is very important to understand timing and not rush or push things. It is also critical not to move in a direction that will take you away from God's will.

We have to be wise. Proverbs 15:22 tells us, *It takes careful planning for things to go right.* Do your research and try to get the best information. If you still don't know what to do, then wait. In so many instances, I have done all the work and have practiced good decision-making principles, but I still did not know what to do.

Instead of deciding, I just wait on God. It is amazing how in waiting the decision will become clear. It is much clearer because other things will happen that will crystallize the situation and make it easier for you. If you focus on timing in your decision-making, you will make better decisions.

TOUGH NUT TO CRACK

You can be certain that in the last days
there will be some very hard times.
—2 TIMOTHY 3:1

I was in Hawaii recently and drove past a sign for the Mauna Loa
Macadamia Nut Corporation. It said they had a visitor center
where people could sample the nuts and learn how they were
processed. I love all kinds of nuts, including almonds, pecans,
cashews, walnuts, and macadamias. I thought it might be fun to
take a quick visit.

We drove three miles off the main road that was surrounded
by thousands of macadamia trees. The visitor center offered a self-
guided tour of the plant, a video about macadamia production,
and a store with all kinds of macadamia merchandise. I learned a
lot about macadamias and how they are produced.

The macadamia is the hardest nut to crack. I always thought
hazelnuts were hard to crack, but macadamias are five times harder
than hazelnuts. They actually have mechanical properties similar
to aluminum. It takes three hundred pounds of pressure to crack
a macadamia nut.

The average person cannot crack a macadamia shell, even with a decent nutcracker. Hawaiians sometimes literally drive their cars over the nuts to crack them. The employees at the Mauna Loa plant put the macadamias in giant tanks with forced air for ten days to soften them up. Even after that, they still must use special machines to crack open the shells. Now that is a tough nut to crack!

Of course, the result is a sweet, buttery, natural treat. You can eat plain macadamia nuts, you can eat chocolate-covered macadamia nuts, and you can eat macadamia nuts in many other ways—including in cookies. There are not many places in the world where macadamias can be grown since they require a certain climate and soil. They are native to Australia and are popular in Hawaii, but South Africa is the leading producer.

Second Timothy 3:1 tells us, *You can be certain that in the last days there will be some very hard times.* Verse 4 says about people that *instead of loving God, they will love pleasure.* These are the times we are living in, and honestly, it will get worse as more people choose to be godless.

Hard times will come for those who are godly. Choosing to follow the Bible's principles and commands will not be easy. Persecution will visit all those who love God. We will need to be tough enough not to crack under the pressure. Christ followers need to be unbreakable and unshakable. We must stand firm for truth regardless of cultural mores.

THE VALUE OF INTEGRITY

He grants a treasure of common sense to the honest.
He is a shield to those who walk with integrity.
—PROVERBS 2:7

I don't know of anything that has hurt the church of Jesus Christ more than people who say they are Christians and don't actually live like Christians.

There is nothing worse than being a phony—than being a hypocrite. The word for "hypocrisy" in the Bible comes from Greek theater where actors would wear a mask to play a part. The classic symbol of the two masks used for acting comes from this definition.

The two masks represent the traditional distinction between comedy and tragedy. They are symbols of the ancient Greek muses, Thalia and Melpomene. Thalia is the muse of comedy (the laughing face), while Melpomene is the muse of tragedy (the weeping face).

A hypocrite is someone who puts on a mask and acts like they are something they are not—much like a stage actor.

Proverbs 2:7 says, *God holds victory for the upright and he guards those who walk in integrity.* It is a fact that life is good when you model authenticity, exhibit character, and walk in integrity. God gives you victory when you walk in integrity. It is good when God is leading you to victory. It is good when God is protecting you and guarding you. It is good when you have character.

Life is good when what you say and what you do match up. Words like "honor," "commitment," and "duty" mean something when you are a person of character. It is stunning to witness people who are followers of Christ, even church leaders, who do not act Christlike at all when dealing with challenges.

The word "character" comes from the Greek word for an engraving instrument. The instrument goes over and over and over a piece of stone or a piece of glass, cutting the image in time and time again.

That is exactly how character is established in a person. It is engraved in you and reveals who you really are. It reflects the kind of person you are. Your character is defined by your actions. The decisions you make and the actions you take over time determine your true character.

Character is much more important than fame, achievements, or wealth. People with fame and wealth can have a huge downfall because they don't have character.

Life is good when you are real, when you are authentic, and when you have character. Living a life marked by integrity is the best way to live.

WALKING ON WATER

Peter then got out of the boat and started walking on the water toward him. But when Peter saw how strong the wind was, he was afraid and started sinking.
—MATTHEW 14:29–30

I had the opportunity to visit the outside artistic exhibit *Floating Piers* at Lake Iseo in Italy. The artist, Christo, created huge walkways connecting the mainland to two islands. The floating piers were covered in bright orange fabric, as were the sidewalks on the island of Monte Isola.

The temporary exhibit lasted less than three weeks and was located near a small town in a fairly remote part of northern Italy, yet close to 1.5 million people came to see it.

The experience of walking on water was unique. I naturally thought of Jesus walking on water. Of course, He actually walked on water, while I walked on a series of interlocking plastic cubes covered in fabric—but it felt like I was walking on water.

I also thought about Peter. Matthew 14:29–30 says, *"Come on!"* *Jesus said. Peter then got out of the boat and started walking on the water toward him. But when Peter saw how strong the wind was, he was afraid and started sinking. "Save me, Lord!" he shouted.*

After Jesus rescued Peter, He asked him a simple but powerful question: *Why do you doubt?* (Matthew 14:31). There is plenty of doubting these days. Many events in our world can cause us to doubt. We wonder if hatred and violence are the norm. We question whether the polarization of our country can ever be changed.

At the Christo exhibit, I thought about what the artist was trying to communicate. The setting was a beautiful lake in the mountains with bright orange walkways glistening in the sun. The message was of connection and possibility.

A boundary that hinders connection can be overcome. The floating walkways were filled with people leaving the mainland to go to the island. The barrier of water had been conquered.

Racism can be defeated. People can connect despite their racial differences. I know this is true because I see it in our church. Loving others is what Christ followers are to do. We can lead the way in our country to show how different people understand and care for each other. Community can lead to unity. Unity is what will defeat partisanship.

If people can walk on water, then they can do anything. The possibilities are endless. What may seem impossible is in fact possible with God. Peter could have kept walking on water; all he had to do was believe it was possible.

Strong winds are blowing right now in our world, but Jesus is right here with us. Things may be scary and confusing, but there is the possibility for better days ahead.

WARNING SIGNS

Guard your heart above all else,
for it determines the course of your life.
—PROVERBS 4:23 (NLT)

Mount Hood is a prominent backdrop to Portland, Oregon. It is also an active volcano. It is eerily silent, but it won't always stay that way. Someday it will erupt again, and when it does, it could unleash mudflows like those from Colombia's Nevado del Ruiz volcano in 1985. In that eruption, twenty-one thousand people died in the dead of night in the town of Armero.

Yet Mount Hood is hardly monitored at all. If scientists miss the early warning signs of an eruption, they might not know it is going to explode until it is too late. To avoid such a tragedy, immediate measures should be taken: three seismometers to measure earthquakes, three GPS instruments to chart underground deformation, and an instrument to monitor gas emissions should be placed at each of four different locations on the mountain.

The United States has 161 active volcanoes. Six of the most dangerous are not adequately monitored. In contrast, Japan, Iceland, and Chile have scientific instruments on all their high-threat volcanoes. There is no question that better monitoring could save lives. Volcanoes don't usually erupt without warning, so if scientists monitor the signals, they will likely be able to forecast when an eruption will take place.

It is vital to be able to detect and correctly interpret warning signs quickly in order to give people as much time as possible to prepare. Near Mount Rainier in Washington, eighty thousand people are in the path of disaster. If Mount Shasta in California were to erupt, it could throw enough ash into the air to halt air traffic for days or even weeks, and could cost billions of dollars in damage and loss.

Why do we not have warning signs in place for these volcanoes? Most volcanoes are in wilderness areas where the use of land is tightly restricted. Installing monitoring sites upsets some environmentalists.

What about the warning systems in your life? Proverbs 4:23 (NLT) tells us, *Guard your heart above all else, for it determines the course of your life.* Do you have warning signs to tell you if something is wrong in your life or if you are getting dangerously close to wrecking it?

How are you monitoring your life? The ripple effects of failures often continue for years. While healing and restoration are possible through the grace of God, the cost of failure is high for everyone.

There should be warning signs in your life that indicate when you are heading down a dangerous path. If those warnings signs are heeded, they will save you, your family, and your community from a world of hurt.

THIS IS LIVING

WATCH FOR THE WEEDS

The servants came and asked, "Sir, didn't you scatter good seed
in your field? Where did these weeds come from?"
"An enemy did this," he replied.
—MATTHEW 13:27–28

Jesus told many stories about farming, growing crops, and
reaping a harvest. He did this because the people He spoke
to lived in an agrarian age in which agriculture formed the heart
of the economy. We live in a different era where technology
dominates and the economy is service oriented. So to understand
some of Jesus' teachings, we need to better understand agriculture.

There is a time of year when some people will plant vegetables
and flowers, but others (like me) will not. Those who know about
gardening or farming are well aware of how quickly weeds can
grow. I recently learned that weeds grow much quicker than the
plants.

That got me thinking about this story from Jesus in Matthew
13:24–28: *The kingdom of heaven is like what happened when a
farmer scattered good seed in a field. But while everyone was sleeping,
an enemy came and scattered weed seeds in the field and then left.*

When the plants came up and began to ripen, the farmer's servants could see the weeds. The servants came and asked, "Sir, didn't you scatter good seed in your field? Where did these weeds come from?" "An enemy did this," he replied.

The enemy of our souls scatters weed seeds. These seeds go by many different names, such as greed, lust, pride, gossip, and many others. They grow to look like lack of patience, lack of commitment, and lack of generosity. These seeds grow more quickly than godly virtues. It takes longer to form spiritual disciplines and habits than sinful ones.

It requires constant diligence in order to grow healthy Christ followers and churches. We must recognize that weeds need to be pulled up consistently, not occasionally. Every time something sinful starts to take root in our lives, we need to root it out. The longer we wait, the stronger it will become. We must also remember who is behind this weed planting—the Enemy.

To be on the healthy side of growth, sowing and growing the good seed is required every day. We must focus on growing spiritually. It cannot simply be about Sunday worship, but it must be a daily commitment. The growth may take longer than the weeds, but the result will be much greater and longer lasting.

The goal of all planting is to have a bountiful harvest. If we keep focused on sowing the right seeds and encouraging growth in a variety of ways, we will reap a great harvest.

THIS IS **LIVING**

WHAT A WASTE!

People who want to be rich fall into all sorts of temptations and traps. They are caught by harmful and foolish desires that drag then down and destroy them.
—1 TIMOTHY 6:9

I once visited Germany's Neuschwanstein Castle. Maybe you have heard of it. Maybe you have seen pictures of it. If you haven't, you most likely have seen a castle inspired by it. Walt Disney was so impressed by the Neuschwanstein Castle that he was inspired to build the Sleeping Beauty Castle at Disneyland, and he made it the focal point of the entire park.

Neuschwanstein is a marvelous example of Romanesque architecture. It reflects the castle romanticism of the nineteenth century. Its popularity is immense. More than 1.3 million people visit the castle each year. You cannot help but be amazed when you tour the castle.

The castle took seventeen years to build, and even then it was not finished. King Ludwig II of Bavaria had the castle built as a personal retreat. The king was very shy. In fact, he was so introverted that he slept by day and was awake at night to limit his interactions with others.

The most impressive room in the castle is the Hall of Singers. Ludwig built the room so operas could be performed, even though he would be the only one in the audience. The castle is filled with paintings of operas, especially those by Richard Wagner.

King Ludwig died under mysterious circumstances before the castle was fully completed. Within weeks of his death, the government opened it to the public in hopes of paying off the construction debt.

Ludwig only lived in the castle for 172 days. He spent less than half a year in his dream home. When our tour guide told us how little time he had spent in the castle, I thought, *What a waste!* He literally spent all his money on something he hardly even enjoyed. He devoted his energy and skills to a project that was never completed.

I think the same thing can happen to us. We can spend our lives trying to make money, and in the process, we can sacrifice our family, our health, and our spiritual life. First Timothy 6:9 tells us, *People who want to be rich fall into all sorts of temptations and traps. They are caught by harmful and foolish desires that drag them down and destroy them.*

Our focus can be on wealth and material goods even though we can't take any of it with us when we die. We can end up using our gifts and skills on things that don't really matter and that have no eternal value.

How are you using your time, talent, and treasure? Don't waste your life.

WHAT IF GOD FAILED?

On this rock I will build my church, and death itself will not have
any power over it.
—MATTHEW 16:18

Every year on June 6 we celebrate the anniversary of D-Day. The
Allied invasion marked the defining moment for the path to
victory in Europe. The Germans faced the impossible task of fighting
in Europe on two fronts. The result was victory for the Allied forces.

Winning World War II would have been unthinkable without
Operation Overlord, also known as D-Day. But what if the Allies
had failed? All military campaigns face this possibility.

Historian Rob Citino has considered what could have happened.
If the Germans had launched a counterattack a few hours after
the landing on Omaha Beach began, using their 915th Grenadier
Regiment, the Allies would have been wiped out. A full-strength
unit would have encountered a beach littered with the dead and
dying, the water red with blood. The Germans would have easily
defeated the remaining soldiers.

Omaha was the central landing beach of the five invasion
beaches. There would have been U.S. forces at Utah Beach and

British/Commonwealth forces at Gold, Juno, and Sword. In between would have been a German-held gap.

Instead of all five beachheads linking up within a week and forming a base for Allied offensive operations against the German army in the West, the linkup would not have happened until late July or even August. This would have left the troops with serious logistical issues of food, fuel, and ammunition.

This would also have led to a renewed sense of confidence on the part of the German forces, along with renewed loyalty to Hitler, who claimed he would smash the invasion in the West—and he would have been able to claim to have done it at least in one spot.

America was in an election year. An "Omaha Catastrophe" could have created problems. The unity of Americans could have been splintered and could have even changed the result of the election. An alternate history where the D-Day Omaha Beach invasion failed would have changed the course of Operation Overlord, World War II, and the entire shape of the postwar world.

An even greater consideration, though, is what would have happened if God had failed. What would this world be like if Jesus had not fulfilled the Father's plan? There would be no salvation, we would be separated from Almighty God, and our lives would lack meaning and purpose.

What if Jesus had succeeded but the apostles had failed? What if they had chosen not to preach the gospel and launch the church? What if Paul had not planted churches around the known world and expanded the church?

Jesus said in Matthew 16:18, *I will build my church, and death itself will not have any power over it.* Thanks be to God, He did not fail!

WHAT'S YOUR LEGACY?

David was rich and respected and lived to be an old man. Then he died, and his son Solomon became king.

—1 CHRONICLES 29:28

First Chronicles 10:13–14 says, *Saul died because he was unfaithful and disobeyed the LORD. He even asked advice from a woman who talks to spirits of the dead, instead of asking the LORD. So the LORD had Saul killed and gave his kingdom to David, the son of Jesse.*

Several chapters later, in 1 Chronicles 29:26–28, it reads, *David the son of Jesse was king of Israel for forty years. He ruled from Hebron for seven years and from Jerusalem for thirty-three years. David was rich and respected and lived to be an old man. Then he died, and his son Solomon became king.*

When many of us hear the word "legacy," we think it is kind of a big concept—maybe too big to get our arms around. But it is not too big. It would be a gigantic mistake to think that the time to consider your legacy is later in life. In reality, the time to consider your legacy is today.

You have a distinct advantage if you have more of your life ahead of you than the life you have already lived. What a perfect time to think about a legacy! Even if you are like me, with less of your life ahead of you than behind you, you still have time to consider your legacy.

First Chronicles gives two very different epitaphs—two opposite summaries of two different people. There was Saul, whom the people wanted to be king. Saul fit every physical characteristic they thought a person should have as king. The Bible tells us that he was the most handsome man in the entire kingdom. He was also the most physically imposing man, so everyone thought he should be king.

However, Saul died because he was unfaithful and disobeyed the Lord. The Lord had Saul killed (he committed suicide rather than be captured), and He gave his kingdom to David.

David took over as king. Unlike Saul, David was nothing to look at. The Bible calls him ruddy, which is to say that he probably had light or reddish hair and freckles, and was not particularly impressive to look at. He was just a lowly shepherd, yet God picked him to be king.

David successfully ruled for forty years, which is a long and impressive reign. After years of leading his country, he was rich and respected, and he lived to be an old man.

Saul's life ended in suicide and disgrace. David's life ended peacefully and with honor. These were two different lives and two different legacies: which would you choose for your life?

WHEN THE PANDEMIC IS OVER

Stop lying and start telling each other the truth.
—EPHESIANS 4:25

Ten years from now when you look back at the coronavirus pandemic, what will you say? Will your memory be recollection or reconstruction? Your accounts of what happened could begin with "It was obvious to me . . ." or "Everybody knew that . . ." or "What I did differently was . . ."

If you do, then memory is reconstructive, built partly on what happened and built largely on what you learned later about what happened. It is based on what you say you supposedly did and how you handled such an incredible crisis.

It is hindsight bias—when after something happens, we say that we foresaw that it would occur and that what we did was nobler, wiser, or braver than what others did. This kind of faulty thinking, however, could keep us from making the changes we need to make while the crisis is still fresh in our minds.

In 1972, researchers asked people the likelihood of various outcomes regarding President Nixon's upcoming trips to China and Russia. We now call those visits "historic" because they thawed decades of hostility between the United States and those Communist nations.

About two weeks after Nixon's visits, 71 percent of people recalled putting better odds on his success than they did at the time. Four months later, 81 percent remembered being surer that Nixon would succeed than they had said beforehand. In advance, no one knew whether those trips would accomplish anything, but just a few months later, they supposedly did.

In 1995, one week after the O. J. Simpson verdict, 58 percent of people recalled predicting that he would be found not guilty. A year later, 68 percent remembered saying he would be acquitted. The fact is that only 48 percent of them had said so before the verdict. After one year, a 20 percent increase in knowledge magically appeared.

Most of us like to see ourselves in a positive light. We want to believe we are smart and rational. We will be tempted to recall our actions during the pandemic as godlier than they actually were. Ephesians 4:25 says, *Stop lying and start telling each other the truth.*

We need to choose faith over fear, worship over worry, and praise over panic. We need to rise up to the challenge and live out what it means to be a fully devoted follower of Christ.

When we look back on this pandemic, what will we say to our kids and grandkids? How will we describe what it was like and how we responded to this once-in-a-generation challenge? Did we run in fear, or did we rise in faith?

WHEN WE PRACTICE TO DECEIVE

There are six things the LORD hates,
seven that are detestable to him: . . . a lying tongue, . . .
a heart that devises wicked schemes.
—PROVERBS 6:16–18 (NIV)

Animals are fascinating. For instance, take the fork-tailed drongo. This bird spends most of the year as a "watch bird" for meerkats and other birds. When it sees a potential threat, it chirps and the animals flee.

During colder months, though, when food is scarcer, the drongo chirps the danger call when there is no threat. When the animals run for safety, the drongo flies down and eats the food left on the ground. He gains the trust of other animals, only to deceive them later.

Meerkats can only be fooled so many times by the false warning before they figure it out. The drongo then imitates the danger call of another meerkat to make them run away, and he again gets their food.

Fireflies trick their own kind with their flashing light pattern. By mimicking the male's pattern, a female from a different species can lure a male. The male thinks the female wants to mate, but she actually wants him to be her next meal.

The burrowing owl lives underground in deep burrows instead of in trees. A female will collect mammal droppings and place them near her nest. When insects, spiders, and other small creatures are attracted to the smell, they come to the burrow. Having fallen for her deception, the owl catches them and feeds them to her young.

This deception in the animal kingdom is part of life, but in God's kingdom it is not. We are to live above all deception and dishonesty. Proverbs 6:16–18 (NIV) says, *There are six things the LORD hates, seven that are detestable to him: a lying tongue, . . . a heart that devises wicked schemes.*

God can't stand it when we are not honest and genuine. He hates to see His followers acting just like secular people who lie and scheme to get what they want. He wants us to be people who speak the truth, honor our agreements, and follow His plan—not those who devise their own schemes.

The Bible makes it clear how much God hates and detests these behaviors, and this should be a huge warning to us. God is truth, and the Enemy is the father of lies. God wants us to walk in truth and have nothing to do with lies.

Practicing deception takes us away from God's best for our lives and leads us into many problems. Breaking trust damages our relationships and reputation.

Always seek and tell the truth.

WHY PRAYER AND FASTING?

When you fast, do not look somber as the hypocrites do, for they disfigure their faces to show others they are fasting.
—**MATTHEW 6:16 (NIV)**

In Matthew 6:16, Jesus said, *When you fast.* He did not say *if* you fast, but *when* you fast. Jesus expected His followers to fast. Moses fasted, David fasted, Paul fasted, and Jesus fasted.

Christian leaders throughout history have fasted. Luther, Calvin, Wesley, Finney, Edwards, Moody, and many other Christian leaders fasted. Fasting is always done in connection with prayer. Fasting without prayer is a form of dieting; it becomes a spiritual practice when it is combined with prayer.

There can be wrong motivations for fasting. Some people fast to try to earn rewards from God. They think that if they sacrifice food, God will grant them extra blessings. Others fast as a substitute for obedience. Isaiah tells us that if we fast and yet do not act right, God will not hear and answer our prayers (see Isaiah 58:3).

Some people fast to impress other people—they want it to be known that they are fasting. They think others will consider them godly or pious if they know they are giving up food. Still others fast out of religious observance. They treat it like other spiritual practices because they think Christ followers are supposed to fast as a duty or obligation.

There are powerful benefits to fasting. Fasting shows that we are putting God first by denying ourselves food. It is an act that deepens our commitment to Christ. Fasting creates a greater hunger for God to work. Devoting time to prayer and fasting results in an unwavering desire to see God move above all else. Fasting brings about a laser-like spiritual focus.

The result is an intensified prayer concentration that is unlike anything else. Fasting injects us with a new energy in prayer. It solidifies in us a greater determination to seek God through prayer. Fasting opens us up to the Spirit's working in our lives. We transcend simple natural desires and move into a new place spiritually.

This should create a healthy motivation to fast and pray. If it seems intimidating to go without eating, start small. Try fasting for one day. You will be hungry and you may feel weak or tired, but the longer you fast, the cleaner your body will become and the better you will ultimately feel. Of course, if you have a medical condition or are on prescription drugs, you should consult your doctor before beginning a fast.

I have fasted at different times for more than thirty years. The positive spiritual impact it has had on my life is immeasurable. If you want to grow spiritually and reach levels you have never reached before, try fasting and praying. There is a reason Jesus expects us to do so.

YOU CAN'T TAKE IT WITH YOU

Their names are now written in the book of life.
—PHILIPPIANS 4:3

I had the opportunity to attend the exhibit *King Tut: Treasures of the Golden Pharaoh*. It debuted in Los Angeles and was taken to ten cities around the world. I saw it in Paris before it went to London and other cities, such as Sydney and Tokyo.

Afterward, the artifacts returned to Cairo, where they are now permanently housed alongside the full King Tut collection in the new Grand Egyptian Museum, which opened in 2021. The traveling exhibit I saw was the last time these artifacts will be seen outside Egypt.

What a collection it was! There were 150 artifacts; previous King Tut exhibits never had more than fifty-five artifacts. The exhibit had sixty artifacts that had never been seen before outside of Egypt. It included the oldest glove and trumpet in the world. There were many other interesting artifacts, including furniture, weapons, and games. There was even a small boat.

The Egyptians strongly believed in the afterlife. They believed that they needed to leave items in the burial crypt that might be needed in the next life, so they put in food, lamps, clothes, and many other items.

The Egyptian thinking was that all these treasures would help the deceased to survive in the afterlife. They even included a golden mask. When Howard Carter discovered King Tut's burial crypt, he found several rooms and chambers and more than three thousand artifacts. Everything King Tut would need in the afterlife was buried with him.

In reality, the afterlife requires no material possessions. We don't need precious metals, jewels, clothing, or boats. As my dad used to say, "I've never seen a hearse pulling a U-Haul."

Only the soul is eternal; everything else passes away. The most important consideration in the afterlife is the health of your soul. You take nothing with you into eternity, and the only thing you need is not material.

Philippians 4:3 tells us, *Their names are now written in the book of life.* We will each be judged on whether our name is found in the heavenly database. Did you repent of your sins and accept Jesus Christ into your life? That is the first judgment.

The second judgment is regarding what you did with your life. Did you follow Jesus' teachings and the Bible's principles?

That is all you take with you when you die. How you respond to Jesus and how you live your life are what determine your afterlife—nothing else matters.

YOU CAN'T LOCK UP THE GOSPEL

I am locked up in jail and treated like a criminal. But God's good
news isn't locked in jail.

—2 TIMOTHY 2:9

I n 2 Timothy 2:9, Paul writes, *And because of this message, I am
locked up in jail and treated like a criminal. But God's good news isn't
locked in jail.* When I was in Rome, I visited the Mamertine Prison
where Paul was imprisoned. It is also where Peter was imprisoned
before he was martyred. The cell was small, dark, and wet. This was
the final place Paul was imprisoned before his martyrdom, but this
was not his only jail cell. He had also been imprisoned in Caesarea
on the coast of Israel, and he had been under house arrest in Rome.
Paul spent more than four years of his life in jail.

Paul had been seen in Jerusalem with Trophimus, a gentile from
Ephesus. Thus, a rumor quickly spread that the apostle had *brought
Greeks into the temple and defiled this holy place* (Acts 21:28 NIV), which
was a capital offense. Forty men vowed to not eat or drink until they
had killed Paul. Paul was a Roman citizen, and his life was spared only
when Roman officials intervened and took him under heavy guard
(470 soldiers) to Caesarea, where he was confined in Herod's palace.

Over a period of time, Paul was subjected to a series of interrogations. After two years had lapsed and it appeared that "justice delayed is justice denied," he concluded that he would never receive a fair hearing under the present circumstances—so exercising his right as a Roman citizen, he appealed his case to Caesar.

Paul was then transported to Rome, where he was put under house arrest. He was confined to his lodgings and handcuffed to different soldiers who guarded him in four-hour shifts. The conditions under which Paul lived should have held back his efforts to proclaim the gospel, but they actually helped to spread the good news. He was free to receive guests and talk with them about the gospel. Because of Paul, the Roman Christians became bolder in their proclamation of the gospel. Amazingly, Paul's influence was such that even those who served in the emperor's palace had become Christ followers (see Philippians 4:22).

While imprisoned, Paul wrote five books of the Bible: Ephesians, Philippians, Colossians, Philemon, and 2 Timothy. The impact of these five epistles cannot be measured. Throughout history, many Christian leaders have been put in jail. Even in modern times, imprisonment hasn't been unusual, as was the case with Dietrich Bonhoeffer during Hitler's reign and Martin Luther King Jr. during the civil rights era.

The gospel, however, is not locked in a jail. Nothing and no one can stop the good news from being proclaimed. It is a force of transformation for all people. Even in a time when religious freedom is a point of political discussion, this much is undeniable: you can't lock up the gospel; it is the good news for everyone who believes.

YOU NEVER KNOW
YOUR IMPACT

So then, as we have opportunity, let us do good to everyone,
and especially to those who are of the household of faith.
—GALATIANS 6:10 (ESV)

A couple of months ago, my wife and I were at a large gathering
of pastors and church leaders from around the country. We
ran into some folks we had been friends with more than thirty
years ago. We had a great time catching up with them, and then
the wife told us a story.

After they had their first child, we had given them a gift of a
Dior baby blanket. My first thought was that we were way too poor
back then to have purchased a designer anything—but I kept those
thoughts to myself.

She went on to tell us that every child who was born in their
family had that same blanket. Then she said they are now having
grandchildren, and their kids want all the babies to have the Dior
baby blanket they had when they were babies. She spoke with such
emotion about the gift that it took me aback. She almost started

to cry as she thanked us for the gift that had been given so many years ago.

Michelle and I talked about it later that night. She remembered giving them the blanket, but I did not have any recollection of it. We both agreed that the gift had a much larger impact than we could have ever imagined. A few days later we were on a plane, and as I sat in my seat, I reflected upon how such a simple gesture could have been such a long-term blessing to our friend's family.

I also thought about how many other times I might have blessed someone that I don't know about. There may have been times when I have said or done something that a person remembers to this day. I can remember times when I think I did something significant or memorable, but I wonder if those are the times others actually remember. My guess is that there are other times I don't even remember that are the ones that may have left the greatest mark.

We never know the impact we can have on another person's life. A small act of kindness, a word of encouragement, or a simple gift can make such a difference. Galatians 6:10 (ESV) tells us, *So then, as we have opportunity, let us do good to everyone, and especially to those who are of the household of faith.*

Be sure to take advantage of the times when you can say or do something for someone. It may seem rather ordinary, but you don't know how what you say or do could have a lasting positive impact on someone's life.

YOU CAN'T CHANGE THE TRUTH

Obey all the laws and teachings I am giving you.
Don't add any, and don't take any away.
—DEUTERONOMY 12:32

I was traveling with my wife a while ago, and we stopped to get something cold to drink on a hot summer day. After we got our drinks, my wife looked around the shopping plaza and saw a sign for a sale in one of the stores. She had never shopped in the store before, so we went in to look around.

She became confused fairly quickly because the sizes were very odd. As she flipped through the racks of clothes, she saw a lot of 0s, 1s, and 2s. There were even sizes like 2.5. She couldn't figure out what was going on until she noticed a conversion chart on one of the tags.

It turns out that in this store, a size 0 is a size 4, a size 1 is a size 8, a size 2 is a size 12, a size 3 is a size 16, and a size 4 is a size 20. Each size also has a half size. For example, a size 1.5 is a size 10 and a size 2.5 is a size 14. My wife and I both thought this was weird. We left pretty quickly because in addition to the odd sizing, the clothes were not really her style.

The more I thought about it, the more I realized what was really going on. If a woman has gained some weight and is now a size 16, she is a plus size in a regular store. That can be hard to accept by someone who was once a size 8. In this store, though, she is just a size 3. How much better might she feel wearing a size 3 instead of a size 16?

What an ingenious marketing ploy! Women aren't stupid; they know what is going on. Still, though, it can make a woman feel good to see such a small number—maybe even a smaller number than any size she has ever worn before.

It is tempting to do the same thing with God's Word, but Deuteronomy 12:32 tells us, *Obey all the laws and teachings I am giving you. Don't add any, and don't take any away.*

There are Bible verses we find hard to accept. Maybe we feel that they are out of touch with today's culture. Why not just change them, or at least change what they plainly mean? Today's world sometimes treats God's Word in the same way as that women's store treats clothing sizes. If we don't like the facts, why not just change them so we feel better about ourselves?

We are told that living together isn't wrong if 70 percent of couples do it, that gossiping isn't wrong because everyone does it, or even that you can skip tithing if you just can't afford it.

But you don't get to change God's truth—you follow it.

YOUR LIFE LIST

What do you know about tomorrow?
How can you be sure about your life?
—JAMES 4:14

I really dislike the term "bucket list." I think that to talk about what you want to do in your life before you "kick the bucket" is a very pejorative way to speak. I prefer the phrase that I coined: "Life List." That is a much more positive way to talk about all the things you would like to experience, accomplish, and do in your life. I definitely believe in having a Life List. You should think about what you want to do in your one and only life.

I recently checked off one of my life accomplishments when I visited my fiftieth state. I have now had the opportunity to spend some time in every state in America. I live in a special country, and being able to see so many sites has been great. I have visited six continents as well. My Life List includes visiting Antarctica, so when I finally get there I will have visited all seven continents on this planet.

Too many people wait to travel until they retire. James 4:14 asks, *What do you know about tomorrow? How can you be sure about your life?* You never know what your health will be like, and there are many other factors that could impact your ability to travel. If you want to see places, do it now—don't wait until tomorrow.

I checked off another item on my Life List when I recently appeared on a television show. I have no great interest in television or movies, but I thought it would be a neat experience to be on screen just one time. My role did not involve speaking, so it didn't take too much acting—but it was a fun and enlightening experience.

Your Life List should include things you want to do and experience, but it should also include what you want to accomplish in your life. I want to write at least fifteen books in my lifetime. The work and effort it takes to write a book is tremendous, but if there is something you want to do, make whatever effort is necessary. Get up earlier and stay up later until it gets done. Put in the work needed to achieve your goal.

Having just celebrated another birthday, I am keenly aware of how quickly life can move. Just yesterday I was a young father, and now my boys are grown men. Just yesterday I was starting a church, and now we mark twenty-seven years of ministry. Make your Life List today, and get started on turning your dreams into reality.

YOUR ONE AND ONLY LIFE

We die only once, and then we are judged.
—HEBREWS 9:27

In the 1990s, scientists discovered something remarkable. They learned that a jellyfish that is only about as wide as a human pinky can reverse its life cycle. The immortal jellyfish, even after becoming a mature adult, can do this over and over again.

Immortal jellyfish are able to transform back into a younger state when threatened by environmental stress, starvation, or injury. These jellyfish revert back to a small blob of tissue, which changes into an immature polyp, and then forms a colony of polyps that produces a young jellyfish all over again.

The process would be similar to a butterfly turning back into a caterpillar, or a frog becoming a tadpole again. It is a mystery how the immortal jellyfish accomplishes this process. Scientists believe it involves a reversed version of the cellular processes that take place during metamorphosis.

These jellyfish are not truly immortal since they could be killed by predators, disease, or environmental changes, but they won't die of old age. Their ability to switch back and forth between life stages means, in theory, they could live forever.

Biological immortality is something human beings do not possess. Hebrews 9:27 tells us, *We die only once, and then we are judged.* We cannot reverse engineer our lives. We do not have the ability to transform into a younger self. We have one, and only one, life.

We only get one shot at this life. There is no reincarnation—no second chance to get things right. Your one and only life must be lived to its fullest. We only have one opportunity on earth, and what we do affects all of eternity.

Now is the time to evaluate your life. Now is the time to reflect on your actions and reassess your priorities. This is the moment to refocus on what is important and realign yourself with godly values. Now is the time to shift out of your comfort zone and into something new.

If God blesses us with a long life, what will we see when we look back? What we do today will determine what we see someday—and if our life is somehow cut short, we have even less time to get it right.

The reality is that life is short, and we will be judged based upon our sojourn on this earth. It is time to make whatever shifts need to happen in our thinking, attitude, values, and behavior. We must fulfill our unique calling from God and live out His plan for our lives.

ACKNOWLEDGMENTS

This book was written differently than any other I have written. It took six years of consistent, small segments of writing to produce the finished product. I would not have started writing devotions if it were not for the encouragement of Dave Jackson. As usual, my assistant, Terri Connell, performed many different tasks to make this book a reality. My wife, Michelle, was my travel partner on many of the journey's I detail in this book. Tour guides, park rangers, and total strangers shared with me many of the stories in this book. Thanks to Esther Fedorkevich, Kyle Duncan, Deryn Pieterse, Hannah Clark, and the Fedd Agency team that made this book better.

ABOUT THE AUTHOR

Rick McDaniel is the president of High Impact Living. He is also a speaker, writer, host of the *Point of Impact* podcast, and author of eight books. He has three earned degrees, including a master's degree from Boston College and an advanced degree from Duke University. Rick founded and pastored Richmond Community Church for 27 years. He is also a regular contributor for Fox News and has written for many magazines, journals, and newspapers. His "Daily Devotions with Rick McDaniel" can be heard on Pray.com, and his speaking is featured on YouTube, Amazon, and Audible. Rick is married and has two sons.

FOR MORE INFORMATION:

www.rickmcdaniel.com

Twitter: @rickmcdaniel

Instagram: @rickmcdaniel_official

Facebook: pastorrickmcdaniel